The CIVIL WAR
2006 engagement calendar
Library of Congress

Catalog No. T223
Published by Pomegranate Communications, Inc.
Box 808022, Petaluma CA 94975

Available in Canada from Canadian Manda Group
165 Dufferin Street, Toronto, Ontario M6K 3H6
Available in the UK and mainland Europe from Pomegranate Europe Ltd.
Unit 1, Heathcote Business Centre, Hurlbutt Road, Warwick, Warwickshire CV34 6TD, UK
Available in Australia from Hardie Grant Books, 12 Claremont Street, South Yarra, Victoria 3141
Available in New Zealand from Southern Publishers Group, P.O. Box 8360, Symonds Street, Auckland
Available in Asia (including the Middle East), Africa, and Latin America from
Pomegranate International Sales, 113 Babcombe Drive, Thornhill, Ontario L3T 1M9, Canada

Front cover: *Assault on Fort Sanders* (Nov. 29, 1863) (detail)
Color lithograph by Kurz & Allison, 1891
Prints and Photographs Division, LC-USZC4-1730

Designed by Gina Bostian

Dates in color indicate federal holidays.

All astronomical data supplied in this calendar are expressed in Greenwich Mean Time (GMT).

Moon phases and American, Canadian, and UK holidays are noted.

NEW MOON FIRST QUARTER FULL MOON LAST QUARTER

The resources of the Library of Congress are particularly valuable in studying the Civil War. The Library's Manuscript Division has an unsurpassed collection of papers of the political and military leaders of the period, as well as papers of soldiers, nurses, teachers, and others involved in the war. The Geography and Map Division has a rich collection of printed and manuscript maps relating to the war. The Music Division has an assemblage of Civil War sheet music numbering in the thousands. The Rare Book and Special Collections Division houses rare Confederate imprints, books relating to the Union, the Albert Whital Stern collection of Lincolniana, and many Civil War broadsides. The General Collections contain thousands of printed diaries and memoirs, regimental histories, the official records of the war, and many other publications. Union and Confederate newspapers are available via the Rare Book and Newspaper and Current Periodicals reading rooms. And the collections of the Prints and Photographs Division are exceptionally rich in Civil War materials—from the original drawings of artist-correspondents, through thousands of lithographs and engravings, to the photographs prepared by Mathew Brady and his staff.

Among the Civil War resources in the Library's collections is *The Civil War Day by Day,* compiled by E. B. Long with Barbara Long and published by Doubleday; it was the primary resource in assembling the information on daily events included in this calendar.

Compiled by Margaret E. Wagner, Publishing Office, Library of Congress. Captions by Margaret E. Wagner, with Linda Barrett Osborne and Colin Wambsgams.

TO ORDER REPRODUCTIONS OF IMAGES IN THIS CALENDAR: Note the Library of Congress negative number provided with the image (LC-USZ6-, USZ62, or LC-B indicates b/w negative; LC-USZC4- indicates color transparency). Where no negative exists, note the Library division and the title of the item. Duplicates may be ordered from the Library of Congress, Photoduplication Service, Washington DC 20540-4570; (202) 707-5640; fax (202) 707-1771.

IN THIS CALENDAR: Alfred Brunson McCalmont (1822–1874) entered the war as a lieutenant colonel of the 142d Pennsylvania Infantry in September 1862 and was appointed brevet brigadier general in March 1865—a promotion he had long sought and for which he transferred from the 142d to the 208th Pennsylvania Infantry. A Democrat, McCalmont was among the many Northerners of the time who were highly critical of Republican president Abraham Lincoln, and his general views on Radical Republicans—who favored aggressive pursuit of the war until the Confederacy surrendered—were sometimes bitterly uncomplimentary. Political comments pepper the wartime letters he sent to his brother, revealing McCalmont's fervent wish that Democrat George W. Woodward would oust Republican Andrew G. Curtin in the 1863 contest for governor of Pennsylvania (Curtin remained in office) and his strong support for General George C. McClellan, former general-in-chief of Union armies, in McClellan's 1864 bid for the US presidency. McCalmont remained in the Eastern Theater of Operations throughout the war, serving both on court martial panels and in the field. He fought at Gettysburg and participated in the subsequent pursuit of Lee's army and in the lengthy 1864–1865 campaign for Petersburg, Virginia. In addition to his political views, his letters reveal a deep empathy for the men of his regiments as they suffered through the losses and deprivations of campaigning. In 1908, his son Robert published McCalmont's letters in *Extracts from Letters from the Front During the War of the Rebellion.*

Sarah Morgan (later Sarah Morgan Dawson) (1842–1909) was 20 years old when she began her diary in 1862. A member of a wealthy Louisiana family, she lived in Baton Rouge as the war commenced, and the diary records her experiences as that city was threatened, taken, and then retaken by the Union army. Three of Morgan's brothers were in Confederate service, and another was a devoted Unionist living in Union-occupied New Orleans—where Morgan and her mother finally joined him, taking the hated oath of allegiance to the Union to do so. Fervently devoted to the Confederate cause, Morgan loved all her brothers and stoutly defended her Unionist brother's adherence to his principles. Perhaps this rift in her own family contributed to her refusal to tar all "Yankee" soldiers with the same brush: she empathized with the many she saw in Baton Rouge who fell ill and died while awaiting proper care, and she noted kindnesses extended to her family by Union officers. Morgan's vividly written diary is filled with details of wartime prejudices, trials, and daily life—and with family sorrows. Within one week, her family learned of the deaths of two of her brothers in Confederate service. "Dead! Dead! Both dead! O my brothers!" she wrote in March 1864. "What have we lived for except you? We, who would have so gladly laid down our lives for yours, are left desolate to mourn over all we loved and hoped for. . . ."

First published in 1913 (the edition from which the excerpts in this calendar were taken), Morgan's *A Confederate Girl's Diary* has been reprinted several times. Both her published diary and Alfred McCalmont's published letters are housed in the Library's General Collections.

CAMP AT AVERY HOUSE, VA., JAN. 19, 1865. *My Dear Brother: The news of the capture of Fort Fisher was announced yesterday by a salute of one hundred guns. It is a very important achievement. The cause looks hopeful.* [Union General Benjamin] *Butler's removal is to me a source of satisfaction. He is a confounded old demagogue and humbug.*

JAN. 20: *We called on General Crawford, who is commanding the Fifth Corps. . . . It is only a month since that corps took its present position . . . and it is surprising how the country has changed. It was then a dense pine forest. Now it is covered with beautiful camps, regularly laid out. . . .*

—Brigadier General Alfred B. McCalmont, USA

SUNDAY, JANUARY 4TH [1863]. *One just from Baton Rouge tells us that my presentiment about our house is verified; Yankees do inhabit it, a Yankee colonel and his wife. They say they look strangely at home on our front gallery, pacing up and down. . . . And a stranger and a Yankee occupies our father's place at the table where he presided for thirty-one years. . . . And the old lamp that lighted up so many eager, laughing faces around the dear old table night after night; that with its great beaming eye watched us one by one as we grew up and left our home; . . . our old lamp has passed into the hands of strangers who neither know nor care for its history. And mother's bed (which, with the table and father's little ebony stand, alone remain uninjured) belongs now to a Yankee woman!*

—Sarah Morgan, CSA

DEC/JAN

Streaming into regiments being raised within each state as the Civil War began, the citizen soldiers of the North and the South were filled with patriotic fervor for their state or region, for the Union or the Confederacy, convinced that their side would emerge victorious after a short and gallant war. A few sober minds knew better. US General-in-Chief Winfield Scott warned that a Northern invasion of Southern territory would take 2 or 3 years and 300,000 men. Ridiculed by many, this warning proved to be both prophetic and conservative (the war lasted 4 years; more than 3 million men served in the Northern and Southern armies). The soldiers who faced each other in clashes of increasing size and brutality shared the belief that they had "certain unalienable rights" (which each side viewed very differently). "I will endure all, till the goal is reached, till the crowning victory is won," Confederate soldier Rufus Cater wrote in 1862. "The resolve still remains," Union soldier Josiah Favill wrote in 1864, "and until the work is done this army will never lay down its arms."

Off to War
Theatrical poster advertising the play *Gettysburg*
Calhoun Show Print, c. 1890
Prints and Photographs Division
LC-USZC4-1446

s	m	t	w	t	f	s
1	2	3	4	5	6	7
8	9	10	11	12	13	14
15	16	17	18	19	20	21
22	23	24	25	26	27	28
29	30	31				

january

KWANZAA BEGINS — **monday**
BOXING DAY (CANADA, UK)
26 360
1862: Federals attack a guerrilla camp in Powell County, Ky.

BANK HOLIDAY (UK) — **tuesday**
27 361
1860: The US flag is raised over Fort Sumter as South Carolina troops occupy Charleston forts.

wednesday
28 362
1862: Federal Army of the Frontier pushes back Confederates at Dripping Springs, Ark., capturing Van Buren, Ark.

thursday
29 363
1808: Andrew Johnson, 17th US president (1865–1869), succeeding Abraham Lincoln, is born in Raleigh, N.C.

friday
30 364
1862: USS *Monitor,* hero of the battle with the *Merrimack,* founders off Cape Hatteras in heavy seas; 16 officers and men are lost.

saturday
● **31** 365
1815: George Gordon Meade (USA) is born in Cadiz, Spain.

NEW YEAR'S DAY — **sunday**
1 1
1863: The Emancipation Proclamation is issued.

GEN. P.T.G. BEAUREGARD.
JOHNSTON
GEN. R.E. LEE
S. JOHNSON.
JEFF. DAVIS.
S.B. BUCKNER.

JANUARY

In 1860, an army of just over 16,000 men protected all thirty-four United States and various territories. Some 300 officers resigned from the US Army to join Confederate forces, forming a core leadership with the same training and combat experience as the leading Union commanders. Jefferson Davis and the officers depicted here graduated from West Point; all served in the Mexican war, side by side with officers such as Ulysses S. Grant, George B. McClellan, and George H. Thomas, whom they would face across Civil War battlefields. Simon Bolivar Buckner surrendered Fort Donelson, Tennessee, to Grant in February 1862. "I had been at West Point three years with Buckner and afterwards served with him in the army," Grant wrote in his memoirs, "so that we were quite well acquainted. . . . [O]ur conversation [as Buckner surrendered] . . . was very friendly. . . ." The depiction of Robert E. Lee, dark-haired and beardless, is based on a prewar photograph. Former US naval officer George N. Hollins was appointed commander of the Confederate Navy June 20, 1861.

(Top, left to right) P. G. T. Beauregard, Joseph Johnston, Robert E. Lee, Albert Sidney Johnston, Jefferson Davis, Braxton Bragg, Simon Bolivar Buckner, naval commander George N. Hollins
Steel engraving by H. Wright Smith, c. 1862
Prints and Photographs Division
LC-USZ62-83942

s	m	t	w	t	f	s
1	2	3	4	5	6	7
8	9	10	11	12	13	14
15	16	17	18	19	20	21
22	23	24	25	26	27	28
29	30	31				

january

BANK HOLIDAY (UK) **monday**

1861: South Carolina troops seize old Fort Johnson in Charleston Harbor.

2 2

BANK HOLIDAY (SCOTLAND) **tuesday**

1861: Georgia state troops seize Fort Pulaski before Federal troops can occupy it.

3 3

wednesday

1861: Alabama takes over the US arsenal at Mount Vernon.

4 4

thursday

1861: Merchant vessel *Star of the West* leaves New York for Fort Sumter with supplies and 250 troops.

5 5

friday

1865: Gen. Grant asks Pres. Lincoln to remove Gen. Butler from command of the Army of the James.

☽ **6** 6

saturday

1863: Three blockade runners successfully break through the Federal cordon and arrive at Charleston, S.C.

7 7

sunday

1861: Secretary of the Interior Jacob Thompson of Mississippi, last Southerner in the Cabinet, resigns.

8 8

Brownell. Entered according to act of Congress in the year 1861, by Currier & Ives, in the Clerk's Office of the district Court of the United States, for the Southern District of New York. Jackson

DEATH OF COL. ELLSWORTH,

after hauling down the rebel flag, at the taking of Alexandria, Va. May 24th 1861.

PUB. BY CURRIER & IVES, 152 NASSAU ST. N.Y.

11.14 x 6 ?

Unable to fulfill his dream of attending West Point, New Yorker Elmer Ellsworth became a clerk and a student of law and went west, eventually settling in Illinois. Ever brimming with enthusiasm for military pursuits, he secured command of a lackluster band of voluntary military cadets and turned them into the US Zouave Cadets, a group that became famous for its picturesque uniforms and precision drills.

In 1860, Ellsworth entered the law office of Abraham Lincoln as a law student. After working on Lincoln's presidential campaign, he followed the new president to Washington, where he proposed the formation of a militia bureau. He also raised, trained, and brought back to Washington a regiment of New York volunteers.

On May 24, 1861, Ellsworth saw the Confederate flag flying over the Marshall House hotel in Alexandria, Virginia, across the Potomac River from Washington. He tore the flag down, but was shot and killed by the hotel proprietor as he descended from the roof. Ellsworth's death, the first of note in the Civil War, produced a profound sensation throughout the country.

Death of Col. Ellsworth after hauling down the Rebel flag, May 24, 1861
Hand-colored lithograph by Currier & Ives, 1861
Prints and Photographs Division
LC-USZC2-2231

s	m	t	w	t	f	s
1	2	3	4	5	6	7
8	9	10	11	12	13	14
15	16	17	18	19	20	21
22	23	24	25	26	27	28
29	30	31				

january

monday 9 9

1861: Mississippi secedes from the Union (second state to secede).

tuesday 10 10

1861: Florida secedes from the Union (third state to secede).

wednesday 11 11

1861: Alabama secedes from the Union (fourth state to secede).

thursday 12 12

1863: Third session of the First Confederate Congress gathers at Richmond to hear Pres. Davis speak on the state of the Confederacy.

friday 13 13

1863: Federal officials formally authorize the raising of Negro troops for the South Carolina Volunteer Infantry.

saturday ○ 14 14

1861: Louisiana state troops seize Fort Pike near New Orleans.

sunday 15 15

MARTIN LUTHER KING JR.'S BIRTHDAY

1862: US Senate confirms the appointment of Edwin M. Stanton as secretary of war.

GENERAL ROBERT E. LEE.
PUB'D BY CURRIER & IVES, 125 NASSAU ST. N.Y.

"I have . . . resigned my commission in the [United States] Army," Robert E. Lee wrote to his sister on April 20, 1861, "and save in defense of my native State (with sincere hope that my poor services may never be needed) I hope I may never be called upon to draw my sword." When his native Virginia seceded, he entered the Confederate Army. By September, he was in action in Western Virginia, where an unsuccessful encounter with Union forces at Cheat Mountain earned him the uncomplimentary nickname "Granny Lee." In March 1862 he became military adviser to President Davis, but less than 3 months later he was back in the field, replacing the wounded Joseph Johnston as commander of the force Lee renamed the Army of Northern Virginia. From the Seven Days' battles that brought the Union's Peninsula Campaign to an unsuccessful conclusion (June 25–July 1, 1862), through its spectacular triumph against a vastly superior force at Chancellorsville (May 1–4, 1863), to its tenacious 1864 defense of Petersburg and Richmond, Virginia, Lee's generally outnumbered army waged war so effectively that it won the confidence of civilians throughout the South and formed the heart of the Confederate military effort.

General Robert E. Lee, CSA
Lithograph by Currier & Ives, c. 1865
Prints and Photographs Division
LC-USZC2-2409

s	m	t	w	t	f	s
1	2	3	4	5	6	7
8	9	10	11	12	13	14
15	16	17	18	19	20	21
22	23	24	25	26	27	28
29	30	31				

january

MARTIN LUTHER KING JR. DAY

monday 16 16

1861: Arkansas legislature completes a bill calling for a referendum on secession.

tuesday 17 17

1861: The Crittenden Compromise, proposing several amendments to the Constitution in order to save the Union, is killed in the US Senate.

wednesday 18 18

1862: The Confederate Territory of Arizona is formed.

thursday 19 19

1807: Robert Edward Lee (CSA) is born in Stratford, Va.

1862: Federals push back Confederates in the Battle of Mill Springs (Logan's Cross Roads), Ky.

friday 20 20

1861: Ship Island, in the Gulf of Mississippi, is taken over by secessionists.

saturday 21 21

1824: Thomas Jonathan "Stonewall" Jackson (CSA) is born in Clarksburg, Va.

sunday ☾ 22 22

1864: Maj. Gen. William Rosecrans is named commander of the Federal Department of the Missouri.

HARPER'S WEEKLY.

A JOURNAL OF CIVILIZATION.

Vol. VI.—No. 271.] NEW YORK, SATURDAY, MARCH 8, 1862. [SINGLE COPIES SIX CENTS. $2 50 PER YEAR IN ADVANCE.

General Ulysses S. Grant's victory at Fort Donelson, Tennessee, in February 1862, made him a celebrated figure throughout the North, which had suffered a number of painful battlefield setbacks during the first year of the war. Thereafter, although often subject to criticism from politicians and the press, Grant gained, then held, President Lincoln's respect by his stubborn determination to pursue and defeat the enemy. After Grant's forces took the Confederate Mississippi River bastion of Vicksburg (July 5, 1863) and defeated the Confederates besieging Chattanooga (November 1863), Lincoln named Grant general-in-chief of all Union armies, successfully ending his long search for a suitably aggressive commander. Establishing his headquarters in the East, Grant led his forces in a dogged pursuit of Robert E. Lee's Army of Northern Virginia, undeterred by a series of costly battles or by Lee's heroic reputation. "A large part of the National army . . . and most of the press of the country, clothed General Lee with . . . [superhuman] qualities," Grant later wrote in his memoirs, "but I had known him personally, and knew that he was mortal; and it was just as well that I felt this."

Major-General Ulysses S. Grant, USA, the hero of Fort Donelson
Wood engraving, published in *Harper's Weekly*, March 8, 1862
Prints and Photographs Division
LC-USZ62-76968

s	m	t	w	t	f	s
1	2	3	4	5	6	7
8	9	10	11	12	13	14
15	16	17	18	19	20	21
22	23	24	25	26	27	28
29	30	31				

january

1863: Burnside's Federal army pulls back to Fredericksburg, ending its famed "mud march."

monday
23 23

1861: Georgia state troops take over the US arsenal at Augusta.

tuesday
24 24

1825: George Edward Pickett (CSA) is born in Richmond, Va.

wednesday
25 25

1861: Louisiana secedes from the Union (sixth state to secede).

thursday
26 26

1862: Pres. Lincoln issues General War Order No. I, ordering Union forces to advance.

friday
27 27

1863: A mass meeting in St. Louis ratifies the Emancipation Proclamation.

saturday
28 28

1861: Kansas is admitted to the Union as the 34th state.

sunday
29 29

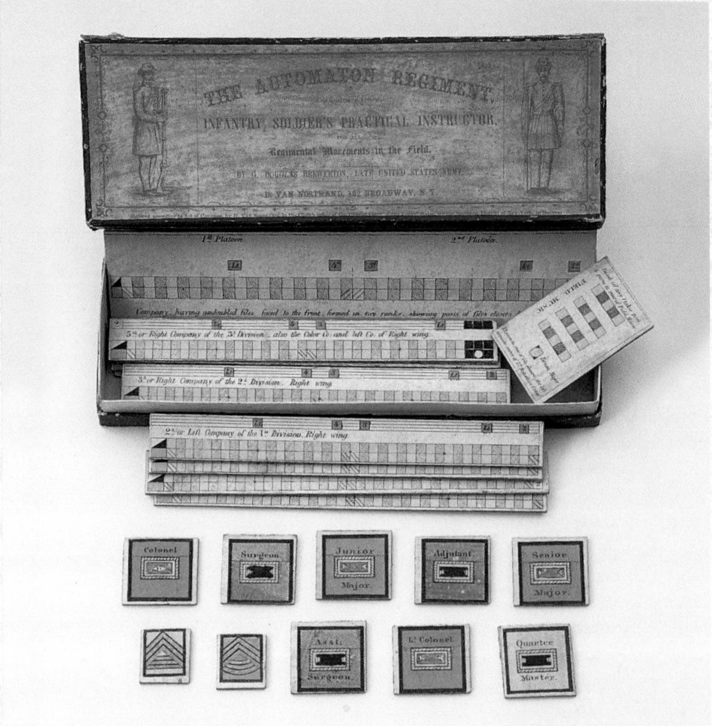

CAMP NEAR BELLE PLAINS, VA., FEB. 4, 1863. My Dear Brother . . . *We are only a mile and a half from the steamboat landing; but our letters go first to Brigade Headquarters, then to Division Headquarters, one mile due west; then to Corps Headquarters, three miles further west; then to Grand Division Headquarters, a little further toward the Rappahannock, and finally to the Headquarters of the Army of the Potomac, stopping, I believe, at each Headquarters about 12 or 24 hours. After going through this interesting preliminary transition they are sent down to Falmouth and thence by rail over to the Potomac river from which they started. . . . [I]t is impossible for a plain man to see how the great and desirable result of getting a letter to its destination is hastened by the process. There is a great deal more of method for the sake of method in the army, than of method for the sake of substance.*

—Colonel Alfred B. McCalmont, USA

MONDAY, FEBRUARY 23D [1863]. *[Here] goes! News has been received that the Yankees are already packed, ready to march against us at any hour. If I was up and well, how my heart would swell with exultation. As it is, it throbs so with excitement that I can scarcely lie still. Hope amounts almost to presumption at Port Hudson. They are confident that our fifteen thousand can repulse twice the number. Great God!—I say it with all reverence—if we could defeat them! If we could scatter, capture, annihilate them! My heart beats but one prayer—Victory! I shall grow wild repeating it. In the mean time, though, Linwood is in danger. This dear place, my second home; its loved inhabitants; think of their being in such peril! Oh, I shall cry heartily if harm comes to them! But I must leave before. No use of leaving my bones for the Yankees to pick; better sing "Dixie" in Georgia.*

—Sarah Morgan, CSA

JAN/FEB

As it became clear that the Civil War would not be the short contest originally expected, a small core of professional soldiers in both North and South faced multiple problems forging disciplined armies from hundreds of thousands of decidedly unmilitary civilians. Marching to war in state-raised regiments, many of these citizen soldiers were led, especially in the war's early months, by regimental officers who were as untutored in military matters as the men they were commanding. Predictable problems arose. Concerted efforts were soon made to root out the incompetent and provide adequate training to everyone else. Regular drills were instituted; many officers studied tactical manuals at night in order to conduct training as efficiently as possible by day. In 1863, artist, author, lawyer, and former army officer G. Douglas Brewerton (whose father had been a superintendent of West Point) published *The Automaton Regiment,* a collection of twenty-three cards of various sizes designed to assist in planning troop movements and to help new Union soldiers understand the basics of army life and battlefield maneuvers.

The Automaton Regiment: Infantry Soldier's Practical Instructor, 1863
Rare Book and Special Collections Division

s	m	t	w	t	f	s
			1	2	3	4
5	6	7	8	9	10	11
12	13	14	15	16	17	18
19	20	21	22	23	24	25
26	27	28				

february

1816: Nathaniel Prentiss Banks (USA) is born in Waltham, Mass.

monday

30 30

1865: Gen. Robert E. Lee is appointed general-in-chief of the Confederate armies.

tuesday

31 31

1865: Illinois is the first state to ratify the Thirteenth Amendment, abolishing slavery.

wednesday

1 32

1864: US gunboat *Underwriter* is captured and set afire by Confederate navy men near New Berne, N.C.

thursday

2 33

1807: Joseph E. Johnston (CSA) is born at "Cherry Grove," Prince Edward County, Va.

friday

3 34

1861: First session of the Provisional Congress of the Confederate States of America is held.

saturday

4 35

1864: Sherman's Federals march into Jackson, Miss., en route to Meridian.

sunday

5 36

RIFLE

AND

LIGHT INFANTRY TACTICS,

FOR

THE EXERCISE AND MANŒUVRES

OF

TROOPS WHEN ACTING AS LIGHT INFANTRY OR RIFLEMEN.

Prepared under the direction of the War Department,

BY COL. W. J. HARDEE, *C. S. A.*

Drill of the Soldier and School of the Company.
nstruction for Skirmishers.

NEW-ORLEANS
H. P. LATHROP, PRINTER, 74 MAGAZINE ST.
1861.

FEBRUARY

Created at the behest of Secretary of War Jefferson Davis and first published in 1855, William J. Hardee's *Rifle and Light Infantry Tactics* was an influential military manual that was reprinted several times. Future generals of both the Union and Confederate armies were well versed in the tactical principles it delineated. The manual reflected changes in battle strategy and tactics resulting from the introduction of rifled firearms (those with spiral grooves inside the barrel), which had more than twice the range of the old smoothbore weapons and could be more reliably and accurately aimed. The advantage in battle now typically rested with the defender armed with these longer-range weapons. Artillery, its crews more vulnerable to being shot by rifled muskets, became more a defensive than an offensive weapon. The cavalry charges and massed frontal assaults common at the beginning of the century were employed much less frequently, for they were far too costly, as demonstrated in the Union disaster at the battle of Fredericksburg and "Pickett's Charge" on the third day of the battle of Gettysburg.

Title page from *Rifle and Light Infantry Tactics* by Colonel W. J. Hardee, CSA, 1861
CSA Collection, Rare Book and Special Collections Division

s	m	t	w	t	f	s
			1	2	3	4
5	6	7	8	9	10	11
12	13	14	15	16	17	18
19	20	21	22	23	24	25
26	27	28				

february

1833: James Ewell Brown ("Jeb") Stuart (CSA) is born in Patrick County, Va. **monday**

6 37

1865: Hampton Roads (Va.) Conference aboard the *River Queen:* Lincoln meets with Confederate peace commissioners. **tuesday**

7 38

1820: William Tecumseh Sherman (USA) is born in Lancaster, Ohio. **wednesday**

8 39

1861: Jefferson Davis is elected provisional president of the Confederacy. **thursday**

9 40

1862: Remainder of Confederate "Mosquito" fleet is destroyed at Elizabeth City, N.C. **friday**

10 41

1812: Alexander Hamilton Stephens, vice president of the Confederacy, is born in Wilkes (Taliaferro) County, Ga. **saturday**

11 42

LINCOLN'S BIRTHDAY **sunday**

1809: Abraham Lincoln, 16th US president, is born in Hardin County, Ky.

12 43

FEBRUARY

"We are required to drill for hours each day," Confederate soldier Rufus Cater wrote in 1862. "No pains is [sic] spared to reduce the troops to a state of perfect discipline. . . . All this is as it should be. The better drilled our army is, the more effective it will be." Discipline held men together in the face of sudden skirmishes, guerrilla warfare, snipers, and the war's huge battles—rending confusions of musket fire, rebel yells, the screams of wounded men, and the smoke and roar of artillery. "You cannot imagine the noise made by a hundred-pound rifle shell whizzing through the air," Union lieutenant Eugene Carter wrote to his parents. "It seems like three or four engines going at the top of their speed, and when it bursts—thunder and zounds, what a noise!" During the 1864 battle of the Wilderness, an area of tangled, tinder-dry woods, another element assaulted the soldiers: "The woods had taken fire in front and now spread to the log breastworks," Union soldier Josiah Favill reported. "As soon as the enemy was driven back we devoted ourselves to saving the wounded from roasting to death. . . ."

At the Battle of the Wilderness
Painting by C. D. Graves, published in *Deeds of Valor*, 1901, p. 476
General Collections

s	m	t	w	t	f	s
			1	2	3	4
5	6	7	8	9	10	11
12	13	14	15	16	17	18
19	20	21	22	23	24	25
26	27	28				

february

monday ○ **13** 44

1862: Federal forces attack Fort Donelson, Tenn., on the Cumberland River.

tuesday **14** 45

VALENTINE'S DAY

1864: Sherman's Union troops capture Meridian, Miss.

wednesday **15** 46

1865: Heavy skirmishing occurs as Sherman's Federals continue their march toward Columbia, S.C.

thursday **16** 47

1862: Confederates surrender Fort Donelson, Tenn., to Gen. Ulysses S. Grant.

friday **17** 48

1865: Columbia, S.C., is captured and burned; Charleston, S.C., is evacuated.

saturday **18** 49

1865: Charleston, S.C., surrenders to Union troops under Brig. Gen. Alexander Schimmelfennig.

sunday **19** 50

1862: New Confederate Congress orders release of 2,000 Federal prisoners of war.

FEBRUARY

Author of the widely used manual *Rifle and Light Infantry Tactics* (1855), West Point graduate William Joseph Hardee was twice promoted for meritorious service during the Mexican War. He resigned his US commission when his native Georgia seceded from the Union in January 1861. Serving in the Confederacy's western army through most of the war, Hardee organized the original Arkansas Brigade ("Hardee's Brigade") and fought at Shiloh, Perryville, Murfreesboro, and Missionary Ridge. A leading figure in the contest with Sherman that preceded the fall of Atlanta (September 1864), Hardee was then placed in charge of the military department of South Carolina, Georgia, and Florida. He could not stop Sherman's relentless advance. Honored by his fellows and respected by his opponents, Hardee was described in E. A. Pollard's *Lee and His Lieutenants* (1867) as a man of "coolness that never failed; presence of mind never disturbed; and an intellect that rose, like his heart, in the tumult and dangers of battle."

Major General William J. Hardee (1815–1873), CSA
Prints and Photographs Division
LC-BH82101-107

s	m	t	w	t	f	s
			1	2	3	4
5	6	7	8	9	10	11
12	13	14	15	16	17	18
19	20	21	22	23	24	25
26	27	28				

february

PRESIDENTS' DAY

monday 20 51

1865: Confederate House of Representatives authorizes the use of slaves as soldiers.

tuesday 21 52

1862: Confederates successfully engage Federal forces at Valverde, New Mexico Territory.

WASHINGTON'S BIRTHDAY

wednesday 22 53

1862: Jefferson Davis is sworn in as president of the Confederacy in Richmond, Va.

thursday 23 54

1861: Texas voters approve secession by a wide margin.

friday 24 55

1862: Federal troops under Gen. Nathaniel Banks occupy Harpers Ferry, Va.

saturday 25 56

1862: Federal War Department takes control of all telegraph lines to facilitate military moves.

sunday 26 57

1863: Cherokee Indian National Council repeals ordinance of secession, proclaims for the Union.

CAMP AT CULPEPER C. H. [COURT HOUSE], VA., FEB. 8, 1864. *My Dear Brother . . . I presume [General George] McClellan will be the Democratic candidate [for president]. The party should not make a nomination too early. In times like these a month may make a total revolution in popular sentiment. If the Democrats nominate early, and put Mac on the track, the Republicans might be compelled to take Grant. On the other hand, if the Republicans nominate first, Lincoln will probably have the best chance for the nomination. I believe, with McClellan, that we can beat either Lincoln or Chase. Grant, too, is probably more popular now than he ever will be again. I doubt whether either he or any other man can bring the war to a successful conclusion this year on the Radical platform.*

—Colonel Alfred B. McCalmont, USA

[SUNDAY MARCH 15, 1863] *Half-past One o'clock,* A.M. *It has come at last! What an awful sound! I thought I had heard a bombardment before; but Baton Rouge was child's play compared to this. At half-past eleven came the first gun—at least the first I heard. . . . Instantly I had my hand on Miriam, and at my first exclamation, Mrs. Badger and Anna answered. All three sprang to their feet to dress, while all four of us prayed aloud. Such an incessant roar! And at every report the house shaking so, and we thinking of our dear soldiers, the dead and dying, and crying aloud for God's blessing on them, and defeat and overthrow to their enemies. . . . There is a burning house in the distance, the second one we have seen tonight. For Yankees can't prosper unless they are pillaging honest people.*

—*Sarah Morgan, CSA*

With two proclaimed governments—one Unionist and one Secessionist—Missouri was the site of particularly bitter Civil War struggles, as citizens chose sides and fought to gain military control of the state. The major clash in this struggle was the battle of Wilson's Creek on August 10, 1861, a fierce encounter pitting 5,400 Union troops under Brigadier General Nathaniel Lyon against 11,000 Confederates under Brigadier General Ben McCulloch and Major General Sterling Price. Centering on a struggle for a piece of strategic high ground called Bloody Hill, the battle turned in the Confederates' favor after General Lyon was killed while leading a counterattack against Confederates who had tried to push Federal troops off the crest of the hill—from which the Federals had earlier evicted Confederate cavalry. Low in supplies and having suffered heavy casualties, the Union troops retreated, leaving a huge section of Missouri under Confederate and prosecessionist sway. Coming less than a month after the Union defeat at First Bull Run, this was another bitter setback for the North.

Battle of Wilson's Creek
Color lithograph by Kurz & Allison, 1893
Prints and Photographs Division
LC-USZC4-1767

s	m	t	w	t	f	s
			1	2	3	4
5	6	7	8	9	10	11
12	13	14	15	16	17	18
19	20	21	22	23	24	25
26	27	28	29	30	31	

march

monday 27 58

1864: Near Americus, Ga., Federal prisoners of war begin arriving at unfinished Camp Sumter (Andersonville) prison camp.

tuesday 28 59

1862: The Confederacy observes a day of fasting and prayer.

wednesday 1 60

ASH WEDNESDAY

1864: Pres. Lincoln nominates Maj. Gen. Ulysses S. Grant for the recently revived regular army rank of lieutenant general.

thursday 2 61

1867: US Congress passes the Reconstruction Act, setting conditions for reintegration of Southern states into the Union.

friday 3 62

1863: Pres. Lincoln signs the first federal draft act, imposing liability on all male citizens between 20 and 45.

saturday 4 63

1861: Abraham Lincoln is inaugurated.

1865: Lincoln is inaugurated for a second term.

sunday 5 64

1862: Gen. Pierre Gustave Toutant Beauregard assumes command of the Confederate Army of the Mississippi.

MARCH

A veteran of the 1846–1848 Mexican War and a former governor of Missouri (1852–1856), Sterling Price was a moderate Unionist who presided over the 1861 state convention that decided against secession. But subsequent encounters with virulent Unionists drove him into the secessionist camp. Leading the Missouri state militia, he joined Confederates from Arkansas under Ben McCulloch in a victory against Union forces at Wilson's Creek in 1861. After a success at Lexington, Missouri, he moved into Arkansas, where his force became part of Earl Van Dorn's Confederate Army of the West. Defeated at Pea Ridge, Arkansas (March 7–8, 1862), and unsuccessful at Iuka and Corinth, Mississippi, later that year, Price (by then a Confederate major general) subsequently helped defeat Frederick Steele's expedition in support of the Union Red River Campaign. In September 1864, Price led an expedition of his own: 12,000 Confederates under his command invaded Missouri in an unsuccessful last-ditch effort to bring the state into the Confederacy and influence the 1864 presidential election in the North.

Major General Sterling Price
(1809–1867), CSA
Prints and Photographs Division
LC-B813-6765

s	m	t	w	t	f	s
			1	2	3	4
5	6	7	8	9	10	11
12	13	14	15	16	17	18
19	20	21	22	23	24	25
26	27	28	29	30	31	

march

monday

1831: Philip Henry Sheridan (USA) is born in Albany, N.Y.

6 65

tuesday

1862: Battle of Pea Ridge (Elkhorn Tavern), Ark., biggest battle west of the Mississippi, begins.

7 66

INTERNATIONAL WOMEN'S DAY

wednesday

1862: Confederate ironclad frigate *Merrimack* sinks the Union *Cumberland* at Hampton Roads, Va.

8 67

thursday

1862: The modern era of naval warfare is foreshadowed as ironclads *Monitor* and *Merrimack* battle at Hampton Roads, Va.

9 68

friday

1863: Pres. Lincoln issues a proclamation of amnesty to soldiers absent without leave, if they report before April 1.

10 69

saturday

1862: Pres. Lincoln relieves George B. McClellan from his post as general-in-chief of the US armies.

11 70

sunday

1864: Red River Campaign begins under Union Gen. Nathaniel Banks.

12 71

William J Jackson
Sergt Maj 12th N.J. Vol.
Sketched at Stoneman's Switch
near Fredricksburg. Va
Jan 27th/63

[January 19, 1862] Dear Father, —I received your kind letter of the 14th this morning, and will try to improve this time (as it is quiet for a wonder) in answering it. . . . On account of the mud, drilling is omitted altogether. Guard duty is about one day and night out of eight; there are seventeen posts, three reliefs to a post, so that each man has two hours on and four off. It is rather tough these cold and stormy nights, but a soldier is expected to stand it without flinching—that is duty. Visions of home, and the loved ones there reposing, during these solitary hours, of course spring up in the imagination, and if a tear comes unbidden to the eye, it only shows that in becoming soldiers we do not cease to be men.

—Sergeant Warren H. Freeman,
13th Regiment Massachusetts
Volunteers, USA

Study of an Infantry Soldier:
The Sergeant Major
Pencil drawing by Edwin Forbes
Prints and Photographs Division
LC-USZC4-4998

s	m	t	w	t	f	s
			1	2	3	4
5	6	7	8	9	10	11
12	13	14	15	16	17	18
19	20	21	22	23	24	25
26	27	28	29	30	31	

march

PURIM (BEGINS AT SUNSET) — **monday** **13** 72

1863: Explosion at the Confederate Ordnance Laboratory in Richmond kills or injures 69.

tuesday ○ **14** 73

1863: Adm. Farragut leads his Union flotilla up the Mississippi at night, past the batteries of Port Hudson, La.

wednesday **15** 74

1863: In San Francisco, authorities seize the schooner *J. M. Chapman,* about to depart with 20 alleged secessionists and 6 Dahlgren guns.

thursday **16** 75

1862: Martial law is instituted by the United States in San Francisco in response to rumors of possible attack.

ST. PATRICK'S DAY — **friday** **17** 76

1864: Lt. Gen. Grant formally assumes command of the armies of the United States.

saturday **18** 77

1865: In the midst of contention with Pres. Davis, Confederate Congress adjourns its last session.

sunday **19** 78

1861: In Texas, Forts Clark, Inge, and Lancaster are surrendered by Federal troops.

Only 17 when the Civil War broke out, Belle Boyd developed a flair for artful eavesdropping upon Union officers occupying the towns in which she lived. On horseback or on foot, sometimes risking her life, Boyd conveyed information to Confederate forces in the early years of the war. Her most famous exploit was warning Stonewall Jackson's forces, during the 1862 Shenandoah Valley Campaign, to advance rapidly in order to cross bridges Union soldiers were preparing to destroy. "I thank you," Jackson said after the event, "for myself and for the army, for the immense service that you have rendered your country today." Captured and imprisoned briefly on two occasions, Boyd was freed both times. Captured again as she sailed for England in 1864, carrying letters from President Davis, she was again freed (and later married her captor). In England she embarked on an acting career, which she continued in the United States after the war ended. In 1886, Boyd began giving dramatic lectures of her exploits as a spy; she continued these performances until her death.

Belle Boyd (1843–1900), Confederate Spy
Prints and Photographs Division
LC-BH82401-4864

s	m	t	w	t	f	s
			1	2	3	4
5	6	7	8	9	10	11
12	13	14	15	16	17	18
19	20	21	22	23	24	25
26	27	28	29	30	31	

march

VERNAL EQUINOX 6:26 P.M. (GMT)

monday 20 79

1862: Stonewall Jackson pursues withdrawing Union troops toward Winchester, Va.

tuesday 21 80

1861: Louisiana ratifies the Confederate Constitution.

1865: Battle of Bentonville, N.C., is last significant Confederate effort to halt Sherman's advance.

wednesday 22 81

1817: Braxton Bragg (CSA) is born in Warrenton, N.C.

thursday 23 82

1862: First Battle of Kernstown, Va., marks the opening of the Shenandoah Valley Campaign.

friday 24 83

1864: Pres. Lincoln meets with U. S. Grant, general-in-chief of the US armies, at the White House.

saturday 25 84

1865: Confederates attack Fort Stedman at Petersburg, Va.; Union troops begin siege of Mobile, Ala.

sunday 26 85

MOTHERING SUNDAY (UK)

SUMMER TIME BEGINS (UK)

1863: West Virginia voters approve the gradual emancipation of slaves.

NOTTAWAY C. H. [COURT HOUSE], VA., APRIL 9, 1865. *At the edge of the village we met a vast drove of Rebel prisoners marching under guard in no kind of order. The road where we met them passes under an arch over which runs the railroad. We had to halt and wait till they all got through. They detained us nearly an hour, though they moved rapidly and were well closed up. Our bands . . . played "Yankee Doodle," "Johnny Comes Marching Home," and other lively airs, while the procession passed. There were 8,300 prisoners in it. To see them coming through the opening at a double quick almost literally reached the idea of subjugation. The Romans passed their prisoners under an arch made of spears, called a yoke (sub jugum). I think the railroad arch is an improvement on the arch of spears, and better embodies the elements of our success. . . . There were a great many of our troops looking at the prisoners, and though there was some joking, I believe there was not an insulting word spoken.*

—Alfred B. McCalmont, USA

THURSDAY, APRIL 30TH [1863] *Talk of the Revocation of the Edict of Nantes! Talk of Louis XIV! . . . Today, thousands of families, from the most respectable down to the least, all who have had the firmness to register themselves enemies to the United States, are ordered to leave the city [New Orleans] by the fifteen of May. Think of the thousands, perfectly destitute, who can hardly afford to buy their daily bread even here, sent to the Confederacy, where it is neither to be earned nor bought, without money, friends, or a home. . . . Such dismal faces as one meets everywhere! Each looks heartbroken. Homeless, friendless, beggars, is written in every eye. . . . Brother's face is too unhappy to make it pleasant to look at him. True, he is safe; but hundreds of his friends are going forth destitute. . . . He went to the General Bowens and asked if it were possible that women and children were included in the order. Yes, he said: they should all go. . . . Penned up like sheep to starve! That's the idea!*

—Sarah Morgan, CSA

Originally named Fort Loudon by the Confederate forces that constructed it, Fort Sanders, Tennessee, was one of the emplacements protecting Knoxville, which had been occupied by a Union force under Ambrose Burnside in early September 1863 after Southern forces had withdrawn. In November, Confederates led by General James Longstreet embarked on a campaign to reacquire the city. Their initial approach was delayed by Union cavalry, who bought precious time for their comrades to strengthen Knoxville's defenses. During the engagement, the cavalry commander, Brigadier General William P. Sanders, was mortally wounded, and the formidable Fort Loudon was quickly renamed in his honor. On November 29, the fort's garrison repulsed a Confederate assault, the Southern attackers held at bay by a 12-foot-wide ditch—and deadly Union fire. Shortly thereafter, Longstreet received news of the Confederate defeat and withdrawal from the hills around Chattanooga and ended his Knoxville campaign.

Assault on Fort Sanders
Color lithograph by Kurz & Allison, 1891
Prints and Photographs Division
LC-USZC4-1730

s	m	t	w	t	f	s
						1
2	3	4	5	6	7	8
9	10	11	12	13	14	15
16	17	18	19	20	21	22
23	24	25	26	27	28	29
30						

april

monday 27 86

1865: Pres. Lincoln meets with Gens. Grant and Sherman and Adm. Porter aboard the *River Queen* at City Point, Va.

tuesday 28 87

1818: Wade Hampton (CSA) is born in Charleston, S.C.

wednesday 29 88

1865: Appomattox Campaign begins.

thursday 30 89

1864: Confederates attack Snyder's Bluff, Miss.

friday 31 90

1862: Pres. Lincoln recalls some of McClellan's troops to help protect Washington.

saturday 1 91

1865: At the Battle of Five Forks, Gen. Robert E. Lee's forces are defeated by the Union army, which now threatens Lee's route of retreat.

sunday 2 92

DAYLIGHT SAVING TIME BEGINS

1865: Confederate government evacuates Richmond, Va.

1865: Confederate Gen. A. P. Hill is killed outside Petersburg, Va.

APRIL

Part of the explosion of men in arms that occurred as the war lengthened, spread, and grew in ferocity, the South's Palmetto Battery was organized and initially funded by Captain Hugh Richardson Garden of Sumter, South Carolina, after he fought at First Bull Run. In the thick of Eastern Theater campaigning throughout the war, the battery contributed to the Confederate victory at Second Bull Run; fought at Antietam, after which the Army of Northern Virginia retreated to its home ground, ending Lee's first incursion into Maryland; returned with Lee to Northern territory and fought at the pivotal 3-day battle of Gettysburg (after which Lee again retreated); and later saw action during the bitter contest in Virginia's entangled woodland, the Wilderness (May 1864). Defending Petersburg, Virginia, during the months-long Union siege of that city, the battery also took part in the battle of the Crater, where an audacious Federal attempt at breaching the city's defenses by tunneling and rigging explosives underground turned into a Union disaster when the North's troops became trapped in the crater caused by the explosion.

The Palmetto Battery, CSA, near Charleston, South Carolina, 1863
Photograph by George S. Cook
Prints and Photographs Division
LC-B8184-10358

s	m	t	w	t	f	s
						1
2	3	4	5	6	7	8
9	10	11	12	13	14	15
16	17	18	19	20	21	22
23	24	25	26	27	28	29
30						

april

1865: Federal troops occupy Richmond and Petersburg, Va.

monday **3** 93

1865: Pres. Lincoln meets with Union and Confederate figures in Richmond, Va.

tuesday **4** 94

1839: Robert Smalls (USN), only black naval captain during the Civil War, is born in Beaufort, S.C.

wednesday ☽ **5** 95

1865: Last major engagement between the Army of Northern Virginia (Lee) and the Army of the Potomac (Grant) occurs at Sayler's Creek, Va.

thursday **6** 96

1865: Lincoln wires Grant: "Gen. Sheridan says 'If the thing is pressed I think that Lee will surrender.' Let the thing be pressed."

friday **7** 97

1864: Nathaniel Banks' Federals "skedaddle" from Richard Taylor's Confederates at the battle of Sabine Crossroads, La.

saturday **8** 98

PALM SUNDAY

1865: Confederate Gen. Robert E. Lee surrenders to Union Gen. Ulysses S. Grant at Appomattox Court House.

sunday **9** 99

APRIL

As Union armies moved into the South, tens of thousands of slaves fled to, or were overtaken by, Union forces and became "contraband of war"; after the Emancipation Proclamation was issued, they were called freedmen and freedwomen. Many settled in freedmen's villages; others were among the 200,000 African Americans who participated in the war that had, for the North, become a crusade against slavery as well as a campaign to preserve the Union. More than 186,000 African American men served in the Union army; 18,000 served in the Union navy. African American women and men served as spies, guides, teamsters, cooks, and nurses throughout the war. "The whole history of the progress of human liberty shows that all concessions yet made to her August claims have been born of earnest struggle," Frederick Douglass said. "Those who profess to favor freedom, and yet deprecate agitation, are men who want crops without plowing up the ground. They want rain without thunder and lightning. They want the ocean without the awful roar of its many waters."

Slaves planting sweet potatoes, c. 1864
Prints and Photographs Division

s	m	t	w	t	f	s
						1
2	3	4	5	6	7	8
9	10	11	12	13	14	15
16	17	18	19	20	21	22
23	24	25	26	27	28	29
30						

april

monday 10 100

1865: Gen. Lee issues his last general orders, bidding "an affectionate farewell" to his troops.

tuesday 11 101

1861: Confederate authorities visit Fort Sumter and demand its surrender.

wednesday 12 102

PASSOVER (BEGINS AT SUNSET)

1861: Fort Sumter is fired upon and the US Civil War begins.

thursday ○13 103

1861: After 34 hours of bombardment, Fort Sumter is forced to surrender to the Confederates.

friday 14 104

GOOD FRIDAY

1865: Pres. Lincoln is shot by John Wilkes Booth at Ford's Theatre, Washington, D.C.

saturday 15 105

1865: Pres. Lincoln dies at 7:22 A.M.; Andrew Johnson becomes president.

sunday 16 106

EASTER SUNDAY

1862: Pres. Lincoln signs a bill ending slavery in the District of Columbia.

One of America's preeminent nineteenth-century families, whose American roots extended back to 1637, the Beecher family included some of the strongest and most influential anti-slavery voices of the Civil War era. Patriarch Lyman Beecher, a Presbyterian minister who believed in education for women as well as men, shared his moral opposition to slavery with his thirteen children. His son Henry Ward Beecher, pastor of the Congregational Plymouth Church of Brooklyn, became a leading clerical voice in the abolitionist movement: the guns he helped provide to Free-Soilers in the disputed territory of pre-war Kansas were quickly dubbed "Beecher's Bibles." His sister, teacher and writer Harriet Beecher Stowe, became the preeminent Beecher of her generation after the publication of her anti-slavery novel *Uncle Tom's Cabin, or Life among the Lowly* in 1852. "I wrote what I did because as a woman, as a mother I was oppressed and broken-hearted with the sorrows and injustices I saw," she said, "because as a Christian I felt the dishonor to Christianity—because as a lover of my country I trembled at the coming day of wrath."

Harriet Beecher Stowe, Rev. Lyman Beecher, and Rev. Henry Ward Beecher, between 1855 and 1865
Brady-Handy Collection,
Prints and Photographs Division
LC-BH82-5279A

s	m	t	w	t	f	s
						1
2	3	4	5	6	7	8
9	10	11	12	13	14	15
16	17	18	19	20	21	22
23	24	25	26	27	28	29
30						

april

EASTER MONDAY (CANADA, UK)

monday 17 107

1861: Virginia adopts an ordinance of secession.

1865: Confederate Gen. Joseph E. Johnston surrenders to Gen. William T. Sherman near Durham Station, N.C.

tuesday 18 108

1865: Gens. Sherman and Johnston sign a "memorandum or basis of agreement" calling for an armistice by all armies in the field.

wednesday 19 109

1865: Funeral services are held for Abraham Lincoln.

thursday 20 110

1865: Gen. Lee writes Pres. Davis, recommending suspension of hostilities and restoration of peace.

friday 21 111

1865: The train bearing Pres. Lincoln's body leaves Washington en route to Springfield, Ill.

EARTH DAY

saturday 22 112

1861: Robert E. Lee is named commander of the forces of Virginia.

sunday 23 113

1865: Pres. Davis describes the state of the Confederacy in a letter to his wife: "Panic has seized the country."

"If we must be enemies, let us be men, and fight it out as we proposed to do, and not deal in hypocritical appeals to God and humanity," General William T. Sherman wrote to Confederate general John Bell Hood on September 10, 1864. Fighting it out was what Sherman proceeded to do. While some of his forces, under George H. Thomas, prepared for battles at Franklin and Nashville that would smash Hood's army, Sherman himself made ready to lead other forces out of Atlanta on what would become known as his March to the Sea. A friend of the South but not of the Confederacy's attempt to dismember the Union, Sherman described his attitude toward the citizens of the land he would be moving through in a letter to Union major general Henry Halleck that September: "If the people raise a howl against my barbarity and cruelty, I will answer that war is war, and not popularity-seeking. If they want peace, they and their relatives must stop the war."

Major General William T. Sherman
(1820–1891), USA
Brady-Handy Collection,
Prints and Photographs Division
LC-BH83-2239

1865: Pres. Johnson disapproves terms of agreement between Gens. Sherman and Johnston: hostilities must be resumed if there is no surrender.

monday 24 114

1865: Federal cavalry closes in on John Wilkes Booth.

tuesday 25 115

1865: John Wilkes Booth is shot and killed; Gen. Johnston formally surrenders his troops to Gen. Sherman.

wednesday 26 116

1822: Ulysses Simpson Grant (Hiram Ulysses Grant) (USA), 18th US president, is born in Point Pleasant, Ohio.

thursday 27 117

1862: At Nassau in the Bahamas, British *Oreto* arrives to be outfitted as Confederate raider CSS *Florida.*

friday 28 118

1861: Maryland house of delegates votes against secession.

saturday 29 119

1861: Members of New York Yacht Club proffer the services of their vessels to the federal government.

sunday 30 120

s	m	t	w	t	f	s
						1
2	3	4	5	6	7	8
9	10	11	12	13	14	15
16	17	18	19	20	21	22
23	24	25	26	27	28	29
30						

april

CAMP NEAR ALEXANDRIA, VA., MAY 9, 1865. *My Dear Brother: . . . I met an officer . . . who has been on special duty at the arsenal lately. He has been in charge of nine or ten persons who are implicated in the [Lincoln] assassination plot. His account of his duties, of the treatment of the prisoners and of their behavior made me shudder. The prisoners were confined in separate cells, and each had a hood or mask fastened over his or her head and face. . . . The masks were not removed even to eat. . . . I should care very little whether they were hanged, strangled or drowned, and I should not have regarded it as a very great calamity if they had been lynched by the mob. But surely it is a great stretch of power and of constitutional law to try these people by a military commission. . . . I am afraid . . . that their trial, conviction and execution will only produce one of those fearful reactions so common in history, when the extreme measures of a powerful and successful administration suddenly change the sentiments of men to horror, disgust and solicitude for their own safety.*

—Alfred B. McCalmont, USA

MAY 10TH 1862. *Early in the evening, four more [Federal] gunboats sailed up here [Baton Rouge]. We saw them from the corner . . . crowded with men even up in the riggings. The American flag was flying from every peak. It was received in profound silence, by the hundreds gathered on the banks. I could hardly refrain from a groan. Much as I once loved that flag, I hate it now! I came back and made myself a Confederate flag about five inches long, slipped the staff in my belt, pinned the flag to my shoulder, and walked downtown, to the consternation of women and children, who expected something awful to follow. . . . Nettie made one and hid it in the folds of her dress. But we were the only two who ventured. We [a crowd] went to the State House terrace, and took a good look at the [Union ship] Brooklyn which was crowded with people who took a good look at us. . . . The kind officers aboard the ship sent us word that if they were molested, the town would be shelled. Let them! Butchers!*

—Sarah Morgan, CSA

MAY

A tactical victory for Joseph E. Johnston's Confederate army, but a strategic victory for William T. Sherman's Union forces, the battle of Resaca, Georgia (May 13–16, 1864), was part of Sherman's deep thrust into the Confederacy that would take him into Atlanta and beyond. Ably assisted by generals George H. Thomas and James B. McPherson, Sherman and his men dislodged Johnston's forces from their nearly impregnable position on Rocky Face Ridge by establishing positions that threatened the Confederates' railroad supply lines. On the night of May 15, Johnston began withdrawing his men via a pontoon bridge over the Oostenaula River and retreated deeper into Georgia. Sherman pushed after them. His tenacious pursuit was a reflection of the philosophy of war he shared with the Union's general-in-chief, who had just begun his costly Overland Campaign in the East, pushing Lee's army back to Petersburg, Virginia. "Instead of being on the defensive, I would be on the offensive," Sherman wrote to Grant several months later; "instead of [my] guessing at what [the enemy] means to do, he would have to guess at my plans."

Battle of Resaca
Color lithograph by Kurz & Allison, 1889
Prints and Photographs Division
LC-USZC4-1751

s	m	t	w	t	f	s
	1	2	3	4	5	6
7	8	9	10	11	12	13
14	15	16	17	18	19	20
21	22	23	24	25	26	27
28	29	30	31			

BANK HOLIDAY (UK) — **monday**

1863: Battle of Chancellorsville, Va., begins.

1 121

tuesday

1863: Stonewall Jackson is mortally wounded in the Battle of Chancellorsville; command of his cavalry passes to Jeb Stuart.

2 122

wednesday

1865: The Lincoln funeral train reaches Springfield, Ill.

3 123

thursday

1863: Battle of Chancellorsville ends with Union defeat.
1865: Lincoln is buried, Springfield, Ill.

4 124

CINCO DE MAYO — **friday**

1864: Battle of the Wilderness begins.

5 125

saturday

1861: Arkansas and Tennessee pass secession ordinances; Confederacy recognizes a state of war with the United States.

6 126

sunday

1864: Gen. Sherman begins his march on Atlanta.

7 127

Its no use talking any more about Chief Bugler for it is an "eye sore and your case" I feel amply repayed with having my life spared and with what I see and here. and wouldn't have missed being in at the battle of Gettysburg for ten thousand dollars not a cent less. but am not over and above particular about being in another of the same style. but if I was sure it was to be the last fight of the war and a crowning victory I would go in happy as a [illegible] we shall probably never see such hot work as long as we are in the service, so be under no anxiety on that score. I am glad that you are enjoying yourself and think it best that you do not go to the white hills. I should think that you had seen enough of Hotel life and if you go to the mountains in style its about the same thing. but if you should go in a little party and put up a farms along the way and have a team and go by yourselves you would enjoy and appreciate the real beauty of the scenery more perfectly than with a crowd of jack dandies silks and diamonds when I come home I will take you and Helen up there and engage that you will have right pleasant time every minute you are there. This place is nothing to Warrenton a barren, sterile, space of flat country I saw no bubbling crystal brooks or springs that the Journal speaks of and the water we have here is of a huff that one of the neutral tints you speak of. as for drawing I draw as much as is compatible with the weather I can write only mornings and evenings and mornings we drill immediately after reville until [illegible] so that we can't [illegible]

we long off in one of the [illegible] if there is any breeze or hammocks slung up in the tree if there [illegible]

You see us in time of stress now

Unless you

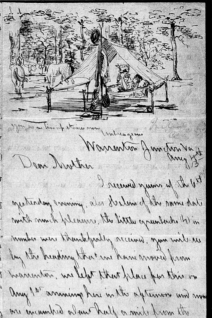

Warrenton Junction Va
Aug 4th 63

Dear Mother

I received yours of the 6th yesterday evening. also Helens of the same date with much pleasure. the little greenbacks (4) in number were thankfully received. you will see by the heading that we have moved from Warrenton. we left that place for this on Aug 1st arriving here in the afternoon and now are encamped about half a mile from the

corps was Walters Regt the 13th Mass also the 12 Mass regt Walter had joined his regt about two weeks previous we spent most of the time together during the two days he was here they had a very fatiguing march coming from Falmouth, I saw several Woburn boys in the Regt and many acquaintances in the different Mass Regts that came through here, the 1st, 12th, 13th. 15. 16th, 19th. 20th, 33d all of Mass, the largest number any contained was about 500 I saw Major Generals Reynolds, Doubleday, Howard, and Hancock, there were others here I did not see Sedgwick was here altogether we have been having gay and lively times here. this afternoon we had a big excitement our Sutler ever since the arrival of the army has been kept destitute of every thing eatable and for the last two days we could purchase nothing well after dinner our Sutler made his appearance from Washington with three wagon loads of stuff and was not half unloaded before an immense crowd had gathered from the 2d Corps which arrived this morning now and then one would make a grab and leave and other growing more bold entered the tent and first thing Mr Sutler knew he was overrun and saw his property on the move, he is a fine fellow and has treated us well, so Captain had our Battery turn out to rescue they marched up and and wedged their way between the tent and the crowd and endeavored to have some order the thing worked well for a while but the the drawn sabres only made them worse, such yelling, howling, screeching, was truly bewitching, our fellows were getting hustled some. the ropes were cut and the tent going over in spite of all we could do Sergt Whitaker made a cut at a fellow who grasped the blow and then wrenched it out of his hand but Sergt drawing his revolver with a threat to shoot him the fellow dropt it and fled but not before he had given Sergt a severe cut across the hand just as the tent was falling and instant demolition was expected General Hays rode up and dashing furiously amongst the crowd with drawn revolver scattering them right and left he was followed by a battalion of infantry who immediately surrounded

our belongings Sutler, the General still ringing around threatening to shoot the first man that remained

the old [illegible]

Centreville June 20th
1863

Dear Mother

I received your welcome letter of the 16th last yesterday evening also Harpers weekly and the Transcript from Helen with pleasure. it is singular you did not receive my last letter to Helen. I answered hers immediately on receiving it accompanied with a sketch of our midnight alarm. and delivered it to the Postmaster myself at headquarters, one day when I was out

W "Why don't some one from home write to me?" Confederate lieutenant James Billingslea Mitchell wrote plaintively in October 1863. ". . . I am beginning to fear the Yankees have come up from Florida & there has been a battle at home, as there seems to be a perfect cessation of all communications. You must not forget that I am always as anxious to hear from home as you are to hear from me." Mail, in both directions, was of vital importance to the millions of Americans, North and South, whose lives were disrupted by the nation's most terrible war. Families hungered for news of their men in uniform; men in the army and navy worried about how their families were coping at home—worries that particularly afflicted Confederate soldiers as Union armies made deeper and deeper inroads into the South. "The accursed invader has destroyed the ferry boats at Vicksburg and at Natchez," wrote Confederate soldier Rufus Cater in 1862, "and we must wait and wait in prolonged, painful suspense till accident, or till the termination of the war shall enable us to get any tidings from home."

Two letters written and illustrated by Union soldier Charles Wellington Reed (1842–1926), who was awarded the Medal of Honor for heroism at the battle of Gettysburg, 1863
Manuscript Division

s	m	t	w	t	f	s
	1	2	3	4	5	6
7	8	9	10	11	12	13
14	15	16	17	18	19	20
21	22	23	24	25	26	27
28	29	30	31			

may

---

monday 8 128

1864: Fighting begins at Spotsylvania Court House.

tuesday 9 129

1865: The trial of the eight accused Lincoln assassination conspirators begins.

wednesday 10 130

1865: Jefferson Davis is captured near Irwinville, Ga.

thursday 11 131

1864: Confederate Jeb Stuart is mortally wounded at the Battle of Yellow Tavern, Va.

friday 12 132

1865: The last land fight between sizable forces—a Confederate victory—takes place at Palmito Ranch, Tex.

saturday ○13 133

1864: Confederate cavalry begin a new campaign north of the Arkansas River.

sunday 14 134

MOTHER'S DAY

1863: Union forces occupy Jackson, Miss.

Deemed "a bold fighter" by Robert E. Lee, John Bell Hood led his Texas Brigade aggressively during the Peninsula campaign, at Second Bull Run, and at Antietam, winning rapid promotion. Wounded at Gettysburg and again at Chickamauga—after which his right leg was amputated—he recovered sufficiently to take command in 1864 of a corps under Joseph E. Johnston. Accustomed to offensive campaigns, Hood proved far less successful at the defensive war Johnston was compelled to wage against General William T. Sherman's advancing forces. Named as Johnston's replacement, he was unable to save Atlanta and then led his Army of Tennessee to smashing defeat at the battles of Franklin (November 30, 1864) and Nashville (December 15). He resigned a month later. "Gen. Hood made us a farewell speech not long since at Tupelo," Confederate soldier Douglas J. Cater wrote in February 1865. ". . . I had never had the faith in him that I always desire to have in a general. . . . I like him for his bravery and untiring energy but he lacked caution and seemed to care nothing for the lives of his men."

General John Bell Hood (1831–1879), CSA
Prints and Photographs Division
LC-B8184-10387

s	m	t	w	t	f	s
	1	2	3	4	5	6
7	8	9	10	11	12	13
14	15	16	17	18	19	20
21	22	23	24	25	26	27
28	29	30	31			

may

1862: Heavy fire from the Confederate guns of Fort Darling defeats a Federal navy effort to reach Richmond via the James River.

monday
15 135

1861: Tennessee is officially admitted to the Confederacy.

tuesday
16 136

1863: Engaged by Federal troops, Confederate forces burn bridges over Big Black River, Miss., and continue to fall back toward Vicksburg.

wednesday
17 137

1861: Arkansas is officially admitted to the Confederacy.

thursday
18 138

1863: Gen. Grant launches the first attack against besieged Vicksburg. It is unsuccessful.

friday
19 139

ARMED FORCES DAY

1861: North Carolina becomes the 11th state to join the Confederacy. Kentucky issues a proclamation of neutrality.

saturday
☾ 20 140

1863: Federal forces begin the siege of Port Hudson, La.

sunday
21 141

MAY

"Never have I seen in New York any speaker achieve such a triumph," one newspaper reporter proclaimed after 22-year-old Anna Dickinson spoke out in favor of abolishing slavery. At 14 she had already published an article in William Lloyd Garrison's *The Liberator.* In 1862 Garrison chose her to lecture for the Massachusetts Anti-Slavery Society, and the following year she campaigned eloquently and successfully for Republican candidates in New Hampshire and Connecticut. Audiences were impressed by the uncommon spectacle of a very young woman publicly speaking about politics and Civil War matters and challenging established leaders. She criticized Abraham Lincoln for his moderation and called General George McClellan her "pet peeve." In 1864 she earned a standing ovation when she spoke on the floor of the House of Representatives. After the war Dickinson lectured on behalf of woman suffrage, giving her talks such provocative titles as "Idiots and Women" because "paupers, criminals, idiots," and women were all denied the vote.

Anna E. Dickinson (1842–1932), USA,
Brady-Handy Collection,
Prints and Photographs Division
LC-BH82-5035B

s	m	t	w	t	f	s
	1	2	3	4	5	6
7	8	9	10	11	12	13
14	15	16	17	18	19	20
21	22	23	24	25	26	27
28	29	30	31			

may

VICTORIA DAY (CANADA)

monday 22 142

1865: Jefferson Davis is imprisoned in a cell at Fort Monroe, Va.

tuesday 23 143

1824: Ambrose Everett Burnside (USA) is born in Liberty, Ind.

wednesday 24 144

1863: Federal marines burn Austin, Miss.

thursday 25 145

1862: Stonewall Jackson overcomes religious scruples and attacks Federal troops on a Sunday at Winchester, Va.

friday 26 146

1865: At New Orleans, the Army of Trans-Mississippi, last significant army of the Confederacy, surrenders.

saturday 27 147

1865: Pres. Johnson orders most persons imprisoned by military authorities discharged.

sunday 28 148

1818: Pierre Gustave Toutant Beauregard (CSA) is born in St. Bernard, La.

Ent'd according to Act of Congress, A. D. 1863, by W. T. Carlton, in the Clerk's Office of the District Court of the District of Mass.

CAMP AT BROAD RUN, LONDON [SIC] CO., VA., JUNE 22, 1863 *[about a week before the battle of Gettysburg]. My Dear Brother: . . . The Radicals [Radical Republicans] calculate that the raid [Lee's movement north, towards Gettysburg] will stimulate the war spirit and strengthen their party. I think it will be just the reverse. Nothing shows more conclusively the incompetency of our men at Washington than the fact that such raids can be made, and that with one army larger than Lee's in their command they allow him to do as he pleases. I am very nearly out of patience. I can see no sign of any change for the better. The President has 60,000 men in the defenses [of Washington] and a whole corps at Baltimore and scattered along the railroad. . . . He could unite these forces and sweep Lee's army out of existence, but he will not do it. He will still hug the main body close for personal protection and blame the Copperheads for the result, because they have denounced the odious features of the conscription law, while he has made no sincere attempt to enforce it in time to meet the exigencies of the service.*

–Alfred B. McCalmont, USA

SUNDAY, JUNE 21ST [1863]. *How about that oath of allegiance? Is what I frequently ask myself, and always an uneasy qualm of conscience troubles me. Guilty or not guilty of perjury? According to the law of God in the abstract, and of nations, Yes; according to my conscience, Jeff Davis, and the peculiar position I was placed in, No. Which is it? Had I had any idea that such a pledge would be exacted, would I have been willing to come? Never! . . . A forced oath, all men agree, is not binding. The Yankees lay particular stress on this being voluntary, and insist that no one is solicited to take it except of their own free will. Yet look at the scene that followed, when mother showed herself unwilling! Think of being ordered to the Custom-House as a prisoner for saying she supposed she would have to! That's liberty! That is free will! It is entirely optional; you have only to take it quietly or go to jail.*

–*Sarah Morgan*, CSA

On January 1, 1863, Abraham Lincoln issued the Emancipation Proclamation. Although it had little immediate effect on Southern slaves outside the reach of Union armies, the Proclamation transformed the Union's war effort—and lifted the hearts of African Americans. The day it was issued, free African Americans celebrated in cities throughout the North. Henry Turner, pastor of the Israel Bethel (A.M.E.) Church in Washington, DC, captured the excitement of the day: "Seeing such a multitude of people in and around my church, I hurriedly went up to the office of the first paper in which the proclamation of freedom could be printed . . . and squeezed myself through the dense crowd that was waiting for the paper. . . . The third sheet from the press was grabbed for by several, but I succeeded in procuring so much of it as contained the proclamation, and off I went for life and death. Down Pennsylvania [Avenue] I ran as for my life, and when the people saw me coming with the paper in my hand they raised a shouting cheer that was almost deafening."

Watch Meeting, Dec. 31, 1862: Waiting for the Hour
Photograph on *carte de visite,* 1863
Prints and Photographs Division
LC-USZ62-119987

s	m	t	w	t	f	s
				1	2	3
4	5	6	7	8	9	10
11	12	13	14	15	16	17
18	19	20	21	22	23	24
25	26	27	28	29	30	

june

MEMORIAL DAY OBSERVED

BANK HOLIDAY (UK)

monday 29 149

1865: Pres. Johnson grants amnesty and pardon to all who participated in "the existing rebellion," with a few exceptions.

MEMORIAL DAY

tuesday 30 150

1861: At Norfolk, Va., Confederates raise USS *Merrimack.*

wednesday 31 151

1862: Battle of Seven Pines (Fair Oaks), Va., begins.

thursday 1 152

1831: John Bell Hood (CSA) is born in Owingsville, Bath County, Ky.

friday 2 153

1864: Battle of Cold Harbor continues. Federal troops under David Hunter fight at Covington, Va., in what will become known as the Lynchburg Campaign.

saturday 3 154

1808: Jefferson Davis, president of the Confederate States of America 1861–1865, is born in Christian County, Ky.

sunday 4 155

1862: Frightened Southern planters burn huge stocks of cotton on the Yazoo and the Mississippi to prevent its capture.

The Emancipation Proclamation provided an added stimulus to the aggressive recruitment of black soldiers that was already under way in the North. Although enthusiasm for military service had lessened among some black men who had benefited from the heated wartime economy—or who had been subject to more blatant discrimination because of wartime pressures—tens of thousands quickly answered the call to service. One of the most eloquent recruiters was Frederick Douglass, who on March 14, 1863, called "Men of Color to Arms!" in a statement published in the National Anti-Slavery Standard: ". . . By every consideration which binds you to your enslaved fellow-countrymen, and the peace and welfare of your country; by every aspiration which you cherish for the freedom and equality of yourselves and your children; by all the ties of blood and identity which makes us one with the brave black men now fighting our battles in Louisiana, in South Carolina, I beg you to fly to arms, and smite with death the power that would bury the government and your liberty in the same hopeless grave. . . ."

Connecticut 29th (Colored) Regiment Volunteer Infantry
Photograph by Sam A. Cooley, 1864
Prints and Photographs Division
LC-BH82201

s	m	t	w	t	f	s
				1	2	3
4	5	6	7	8	9	10
11	12	13	14	15	16	17
18	19	20	21	22	23	24
25	26	27	28	29	30	

june

monday 5 156

1864: Confederate Brig. Gen. William E. "Grumble" Jones is killed in an engagement with Federal troops in the Shenandoah Valley.

tuesday 6 157

1862: Crowds line the bluffs of the Mississippi at Memphis to witness the last "fleet action" of the war on the rivers.

wednesday 7 158

1863: Union troops burn and sack the Brierfield Plantation of Jefferson Davis and his brother Joseph.

thursday 8 159

1862: Stonewall Jackson's troops fight off a Federal attack in the Battle of Cross Keys, Va.

friday 9 160

1863: Troopers under Jeb Stuart meet Alfred Pleasonton's Union cavalry at Brandy Station, Va.—greatest cavalry battle on American soil.

saturday 10 161

1863: Off Cape Henry, Va., the steamer *Maple Leaf* is run ashore by the rebel prisoners it carries; they escape.

sunday 11 162

1861: Pro-Union Virginia delegates meet at Wheeling to organize a pro-Union government that eventually will become the state of West Virginia.

Born in Virginia, William Lewis Cabell resigned from the United States Army in the spring of 1861 to become a Confederate officer. After serving as chief quartermaster under P. G. T. Beauregard in the east, he was promoted to brigadier general and reassigned to the Trans-Mississippi Department. On April 18, 1864, Cabell and his Arkansas Brigade were part of a force of 3,400 Confederates that encountered 1,200 Union troops who were on a foraging expedition at Poison Springs, Arkansas. The Southerners defeated the Federals, but their victory was tainted by charges of murder: more than half of the Union casualties were members of the First Kansas Colored Volunteers, and witnesses reported that some of these men were killed after they had surrendered or as they lay wounded. Although Confederates denied the charge, evidence supported it. Two weeks later, during another engagement in Arkansas, members of the Second Kansas Colored Volunteers shouted "Remember Poison Springs!" as they overwhelmed a Confederate battery.

Brigadier General William Lewis Cabell (1827–1916), CSA
Prints and Photographs Division
LC-BH83-637

s	m	t	w	t	f	s
				1	2	3
4	5	6	7	8	9	10
11	12	13	14	15	16	17
18	19	20	21	22	23	24
25	26	27	28	29	30	

june

monday 12 163

1862: Jeb Stuart's cavalry begins a spectacular 4-day reconnaissance that develops into a ride completely around the opposing Federal army.

tuesday 13 164

1861: The Confederate states observe a fast day, by proclamation of Pres. Davis, to dramatize the needed war effort.

FLAG DAY

wednesday 14 165

1811: Harriet Beecher Stowe, author of *Uncle Tom's Cabin,* is born in Litchfield, Conn.

thursday 15 166

1862: Jeb Stuart arrives triumphant in Richmond to tell Lee of his cavalry's ride around McClellan's forces on the Virginia Peninsula.

friday 16 167

1862: Federal troops under Brig. Gen. H. W. Benham fail in a costly attack on Confederate works at Secessionville, S.C.

saturday 17 168

1862: Braxton Bragg succeeds Gen. Beauregard as commander of the Western Department of the Confederate Army.

FATHER'S DAY

sunday 18 169

1862: Northern troops occupy the strategically valuable Cumberland Gap.

JUNE

A graduate of Harvard University and a physician schooled in the United States and France, Edward Augustus Wild had served as a medical officer with the Turkish army during the Crimean War but chose to lead frontline combat troops as a Union Civil War officer. Severely wounded at Seven Pines during the 1862 Peninsula campaign and again while leading the 35th Massachusetts regiment at South Mountain (a wound resulting in the loss of his left arm), Wild became a brigadier general of volunteers in April 1863. A fervent abolitionist, he actively recruited black soldiers for new US regiments as well as white officers to lead them (including James C. Beecher, half-brother of Harriet Beecher Stowe). He then took command of Wild's African Brigade, composed of the 55th Massachusetts Volunteers (Colored) and the 2d and 3d North Carolina Colored Volunteers (later the 36th and 37th Regiments, US Colored Troops). The brigade served in the hotly contested area around Charleston, South Carolina; participated in the campaign for Petersburg, Virginia; and ended the war as part of the force occupying the former Confederate capital of Richmond.

Brigadier General Edward Augustus Wild (1825–1891), USA
Steel engraving by A. H. Ritchie
Prints and Photographs Division
LC-USZ62-84332

s	m	t	w	t	f	s
				1	2	3
4	5	6	7	8	9	10
11	12	13	14	15	16	17
18	19	20	21	22	23	24
25	26	27	28	29	30	

june

monday
1862: Pres. Lincoln signs into law a measure prohibiting slavery in the territories of the United States.
19 170

tuesday
1863: By presidential proclamation, West Virginia is admitted to the Union as the 35th state.
20 171

wednesday
SUMMER SOLSTICE 12:26 P.M. (GMT)
1863: Heavy skirmishing marks Lee's advance northward, with engagements at several locations in Virginia and at Frederick, Md.
21 172

thursday
1862: Thirty Sisters of Charity arrive at Fort Monroe, Va., to minister to the sick and wounded of the Army of the Potomac.
22 173

friday
1861: Federal balloonist Thaddeus Lowe observes and maps Confederate lines over northern Virginia.
23 174

saturday
1861: Two US gunboats shell Confederate positions at Mathias Point, Va.
24 175

sunday
1864: At Petersburg, Federal engineers begin digging a tunnel toward the Confederate lines via which they hope to blow apart the Southern earthworks.
● **25** 176

CAMP NEAR BOONSBORO, MD., THURSDAY, JULY 9, 1863. *My Dear Brother: . . . Our march on Monday morning lay over a part of the [Gettysburg] battlefield. . . . The trees were shattered by shot and shell. Wheat fields were trodden down. War had done its work; and the air was terribly offensive with the odor of thousands of rotting bodies. It was a relief to reach the outside of the terrible scene, to come again among beautiful farms, and through fields of ripe grain, and at last to reach Emmettsburg. . . . Early on Wednesday morning we started again and marched to Middletown through a drenching rain. Last October our regiment marched through the same town with new clothes, new colors, and a fine band playing national airs. Then we had nine hundred men. Now we have less than a hundred, Colonel, Major, Adjutant, all gone. Then the people were waving flags and our men were cheering. Now the poor fellows left are too tired to raise more than a faint hurrah, and are tramping through the mud wet to the skin.*

–Alfred B. McCalmont, USA

JULY 29TH [1862]. *This town [Union-occupied Baton Rouge], with its ten thousand soldiers, is more quiet than it was with the old population of seven thousand citizens. . . . These poor soldiers are dying awfully. Thirteen went yesterday. On Sunday the boats discharged hundreds of sick at our landing. Some lay there all the afternoon in the hot sun, waiting for the wagon to carry them to the hospital, which task occupied the whole evening. In the mean time these poor wretches lay uncovered on the ground, in every stage of sickness. . . . Oh, I wish these poor men were safe in their own land! It is heartbreaking to see them die here like dogs, with no one to say Godspeed. The Catholic priest went to see some, sometime ago, and going near one who lay in bed, said some kind thing, when the man burst into tears and cried, "Thank God, I have heard one kind word before I die!" In a few minutes the poor wretch was dead.*

–Sarah Morgan, CSA

Friday, July 3rd [1863]. A terrific cannonade took place. . . . We had 120 pieces of artillery on one ridge; 400 pieces were firing at the same time. Skirmishing and occasional firing was kept up until 1 P.M., when the attack was furiously renewed and we drove the enemy from their works, but our supports were not near enough and the enemy rallied and regained them. Pickett's division took the hill on the right, but Pettigrew failed to sustain him. We were repulsed on all sides. . . . Our loss was very great, the men fighting with desperation and great valor. Many were killed and wounded. . . . The Generals had a council at General A. P. Hill's headquarters on the Cashtown Road, about sun-down, and decided to fall back. . . . I met Pickett's Division, returning after the battle . . . no officers and all protesting that they had been completely cut up. A general movement of wagons, wounded, prisoners, etc., took place to the rear, and the unmistakable signs of a retreat were plentiful. There was a general feeling of despondency in the army at our great losses, though the battle is regarded as a drawn one.

—Major Jedediah Hotchkiss, CSA,
diary entry describing the third day
of the battle of Gettysburg

Pickett's Charge at Gettysburg
Painting by C. D. Graves, published in *Deeds of Valor*, 1901, p. 272
General Collections

s	m	t	w	t	f	s
						1
2	3	4	5	6	7	8
9	10	11	12	13	14	15
16	17	18	19	20	21	22
23	24	25	26	27	28	29
30	31					

july

monday 26 177

1863: Confederate Gen. Early and some of his command enter Gettysburg, Pa.

tuesday 27 178

1864: Battle of Kennesaw Mountain, Ga., results in Confederate victory, temporarily checking Sherman's march to Atlanta.

wednesday 28 179

1863: Gen. Lee diverts Confederate forces from an intended drive on Harrisburg, Pa., to march them toward Gettysburg.

thursday 29 180

1862: Union troops, driven from Savage's Station east of Richmond, are forced to leave 2,500 sick and wounded behind.

friday 30 181

1865: All eight alleged Lincoln assassination conspirators are found guilty.

saturday 1 182

CANADA DAY (CANADA)

1863: Battle of Gettysburg begins.

sunday 2 183

1863: Battle of Gettysburg continues as Confederates unsuccessfully attempt to overrun Little Round Top and Big Round Top.

Sometimes called "a damned old goggle-eyed snapping turtle" by his men because of his hair-trigger temper, career soldier George Gordon Meade (West Point, 1835) was also known as "Old Reliable" for his steadfastness in combat and his competence in command. Assigned at the beginning of the war to the defense of Washington, DC, Meade served under McClellan during the Peninsula campaign and was severely wounded at Frayser's Farm during the Seven Days battles. Only partially recovered, he fought at Second Bull Run, was commended for his action at South Mountain (September 1862), and showed such initiative and insight during the battle of Chancellorsville (May 1863) that two of his fellow officers recommended him as the next commander of the Army of the Potomac. He was, in fact, ordered to replace General Hooker only 3 days before the battle of Gettysburg. Successful in this decisive encounter—though criticized for failing to press Lee afterward—Meade remained in command of the Army of the Potomac for the rest of the war.

Major General George Gordon Meade (1815–1872), USA
Photograph by the Brady National Photographic Art Gallery
Prints and Photographs Division
LC-B8172-1467

s	m	t	w	t	f	s
						1
2	3	4	5	6	7	8
9	10	11	12	13	14	15
16	17	18	19	20	21	22
23	24	25	26	27	28	29
30	31					

july

CANADA DAY OBSERVED (CANADA)

monday 3 184

1863: Battle of Gettysburg ends in Confederate defeat.

INDEPENDENCE DAY

tuesday 4 185

1863: Vicksburg surrenders to Union forces, giving the Union control of the Mississippi River.

wednesday 5 186

1801: David Glasgow Farragut (USN), first person in US history to hold the rank of admiral, is born in Knoxville, Tenn.

thursday 6 187

1863: Fighting occurs at Boonsborough, Hagerstown, and Williamsport, Md., as Lee withdraws from Gettysburg.

friday 7 188

1864: Federal troops and militia hurry toward Washington and Maryland to protect the North and its capital from Jubal Early's "invading army."

saturday 8 189

1863: Confederates unconditionally surrender Port Hudson, La., last Confederate garrison on the Mississippi.

sunday 9 190

1864: The Battle of Monocacy, Md.: 7,000 Federals under Lew Wallace delay 15,000 Confederates under Jubal Early as they approach Washington.

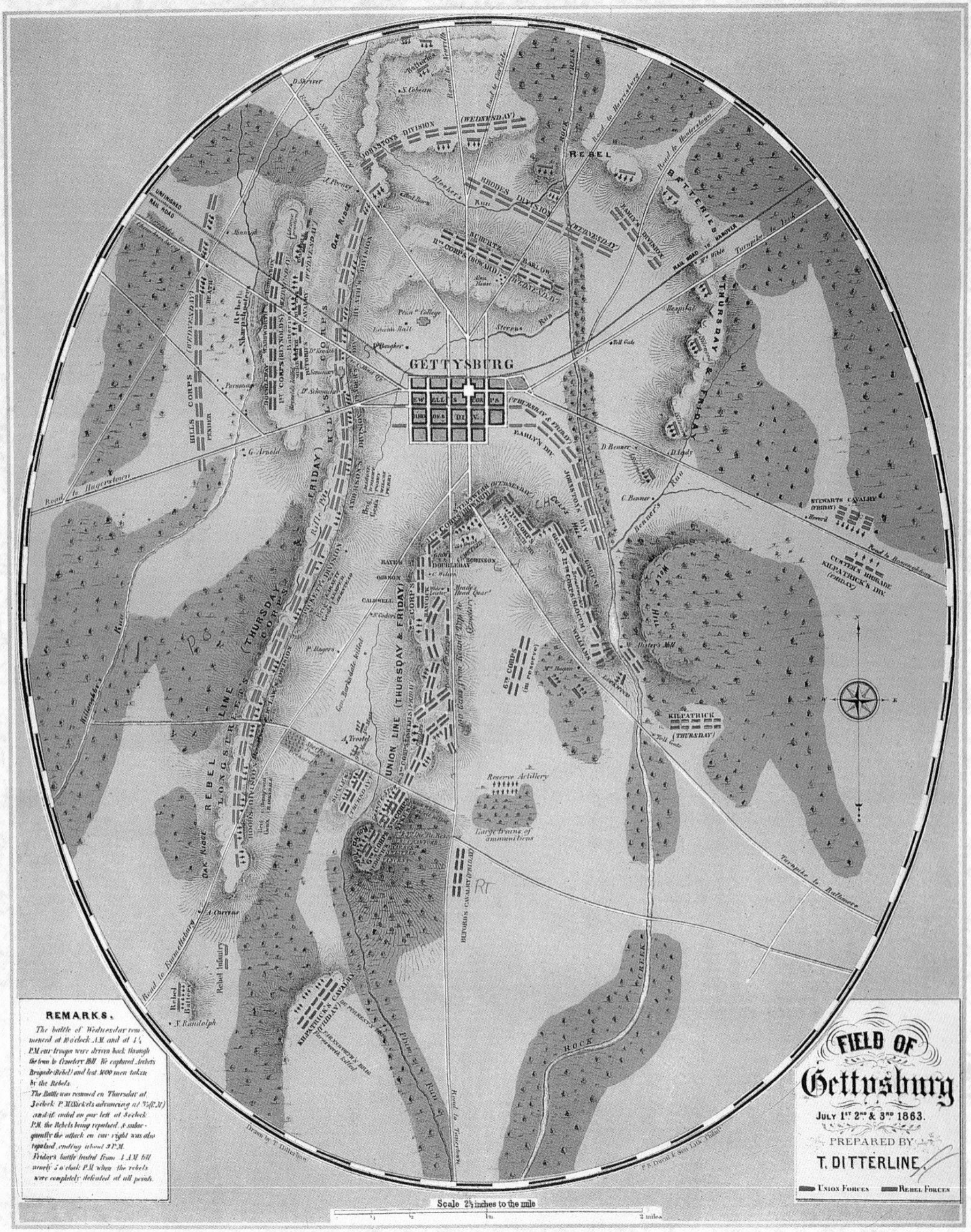

FIELD OF
Gettysburg
JULY 1ST 2ND & 3RD 1863.
PREPARED BY
T. DITTERLINE.
Union Forces
Rebel Forces
Scale 2½ inches to the mile
2 miles
REMARKS.
The battle of Wednesday commenced at 10 o'clock A.M. and at 4½ P.M. our troops were driven back through the town to Cemetery Hill. We captured Archers Brigade (Rebel) and lost 3000 men taken by the Rebels.
The Battle was resumed on Thursday at 3 o'clock P.M. Sickels advancing at 3½ (P.M.) and it ended on our left at 8 o'clock P.M. the Rebels being repulsed, & subsequently the attack on our right was also repulsed, ending about 9 P.M.
Friday's battle lasted from 4 A.M. till nearly 5 o'clock P.M. when the rebels were completely defeated at all points.
GETTYSBURG
EWELL'S CORPS
JOHNSTON'S DIVISION
(WEDNESDAY)
RHODES DIVISION
REBEL
BATTERIES
HILLS CORPS
(WEDNESDAY)
REBEL LINE
LONGSTREET'S CORPS
(THURSDAY)
UNION LINE
(THURSDAY & FRIDAY)
(THURSDAY & FRIDAY)
EARLY'S DIV.
JOHNSTON'S DIV.
6TH CORPS
(in reserve)
KILPATRICK
(THURSDAY)
STEWARTS CAVALRY
(FRIDAY)
CUSTER'S BRIGADE
KILPATRICK'S DIV.
(FRIDAY)
Reserve Artillery
Large trains of ammunitions
KILPATRICK'S CAVALRY
(FRIDAY)
BUFORD'S CAVALRY
OAK RIDGE
Rebel Battery
Rebel Infantry
Road to Hagerstown
Road to Emmettsburg
Road to Taneytown
Turnpike to Baltimore
Turnpike to York
Road to Hanover
Road to Harrisburg
Road to Carlisle
Road to Newville
Road to Shippensburg
Road to Bonaughtown
Rock Creek
Plum Run
Willoughby Run
Benner's Run
Stevens Run
Rebels Sharpshooters
Penn. College
Meade's Head Quar.
Culps Hill
Wolf Hill
Round Top
Drawn by T. Ditterline
P. S. Duval & Son Lith. Phila.

The Union's Army of the Potomac had been placed in the hands of a new commander, General George Gordon Meade, only days before it faced Lee's Army of Northern Virginia in the 3-day battle at Gettysburg, Pennsylvania, one of the crucial turning points of the Civil War. Gettysburg had not been a deliberate choice as a battlefield, but once the two forces engaged on the morning of July 1, 1863, Meade was able to bring the main body of his army into a strong, fishhook-shaped line in front of Gettysburg and extending south along Cemetery Ridge as circumstances delayed the Confederates' two main attacks. When the attacks occurred—late on July 2 when Longstreet's corps attempted to turn the Federal left wing as diversionary attacks plagued their right, and on July 3 with a concerted assault on the Union center (subsequently known as "Pickett's Charge")—Mead's shaken forces held fast. Lee began a withdrawal toward the Potomac River and was soon back in Virginia.

Field of Gettysburg
Map by Theodore Ditterline, 1863
Geography and Map Division

s	m	t	w	t	f	s
						1
2	3	4	5	6	7	8
9	10	11	12	13	14	15
16	17	18	19	20	21	22
23	24	25	26	27	28	29
30	31					

july

monday 10 191

1863: Federal forces land on Morris Island near Charleston, S.C., and begin a siege of Fort Wagner that will last until September.

tuesday 11 192

1864: Confederates under Jubal Early invade the suburbs of Washington.

wednesday 12 193

BANK HOLIDAY (N. IRELAND)

1864: As Federal reinforcements arrive at Washington, Jubal Early begins withdrawing his Confederate troops.

thursday 13 194

1821: Nathan Bedford Forrest (CSA) is born in Chapel Hill, Tenn.

friday 14 195

1861: Blockade of Wilmington, N.C., begins.

saturday 15 196

1862: Newly completed Confederate ironclad *Arkansas* meets Federal vessels in the Yazoo north of Vicksburg, badly damaging three of them.

sunday 16 197

1863: Confederates under Joseph E. Johnston abandon Jackson, Miss., to Sherman's Federals.

West Point graduate George Pickett served in Texas, Virginia, and Washington Territory before resigning his US commission in 1861 to enter the Confederate army as a colonel. By October 1862, after fighting in the Seven Days campaign, he had been promoted to major general and placed in command of a Virginia division that participated in the battle of Fredericksburg 2 months later. Not among the most distinguished Civil War generals, Pickett is remembered chiefly for a massive frontal assault by some 13,000 Confederates against Union lines at Gettysburg on July 3, 1863, that was spearheaded by his division. The costly failure of "Pickett's Charge" marked the end of that pivotal 3-day battle and of Lee's second invasion of Northern territory. "It is all over now," Pickett wrote to his fiancée on July 4. "Many of us are prisoners, many are dead, many wounded, bleeding and dying. Your soldier lives and mourns and but for you, my darling, he would rather be back there with his dead, to sleep for all time in an unknown grave."

General George E. Pickett (1825–1875), CSA
Brady-Handy Collection,
Prints and Photographs Division
LC-BH83-3754

s	m	t	w	t	f	s
						1
2	3	4	5	6	7	8
9	10	11	12	13	14	15
16	17	18	19	20	21	22
23	24	25	26	27	28	29
30	31					

july

monday
17 198

1864: Jefferson Davis relieves Joseph E. Johnston of command of the Confederate Army and Department of Tennessee and replaces him with John Bell Hood.

tuesday
18 199

1863: Federal Maj. Gen. John G. Foster assumes command of the Department of Virginia and North Carolina.

wednesday
19 200

1862: Confederates raid Brownsville, Tenn.

thursday
20 201

1864: Gen. John Bell Hood fails his first big test of command as Southern forces are defeated at the Battle of Peachtree Creek, Ga.

friday
21 202

1861: Union Gen. Irvin McDowell is defeated at First Battle of Bull Run, Manassas, Va.

saturday
22 203

1864: Union Gen. James B. McPherson is killed during the Battle of Atlanta.

sunday
23 204

1862: Maj. Gen. Henry Wager Halleck assumes command of the armies of the United States.

S E Bucklin

"Everywhere were evidences of mortal combat, everywhere wounded men were lying in the streets on heaps of blood-stained straw, everywhere there was hurry and confusion, while soldiers were groaning and suffering," wrote Union nurse Sophronia Bucklin about her arrival in Gettysburg, Pennsylvania, after one of the pivotal battles of the Civil War. There she "washed agonized faces, combed out matted hair, [and] bandaged slight wounds." A seamstress in Auburn, New York, before the war, Bucklin signed on as an army nurse despite being older than the requisite 35 to 50 years. She served in a field hospital at Gettysburg, at Stoneman's Cavalry Hospital in Washington, DC, and near Petersburg, Virginia, witnessing death and enduring harsh conditions. In 1869, she published a memoir, *In Hospital and Camp: A Woman's Record of Thrilling Incidents Among the Wounded in the Late War.* It is a testament to the courage and determination of women such as Bucklin who overcame the mid-nineteenth-century prejudice against women serving as nurses near the battlefield.

Sophronia E. Bucklin [dates unknown], USA
Engraving by J. C. Buttre, from *In Hospital and Camp* by Sophronia E. Bucklin, 1869
General Collections

s	m	t	w	t	f	s
						1
2	3	4	5	6	7	8
9	10	11	12	13	14	15
16	17	18	19	20	21	22
23	24	25	26	27	28	29
30	31					

july

monday 24 205

1864: Confederate forces under Jubal Early inflict heavy losses at the Second Battle of Kernstown, Va.

tuesday 25 206

1864: Early's Confederates follow retreating Federals to Bunker Hill, Va., where fighting erupts.

wednesday 26 207

1863: Confederate raider John Hunt Morgan surrenders his exhausted force of 364 men at Salineville, Ohio. Morgan and officers are sent to Ohio State Penitentiary.

thursday 27 208

1861: Maj. Gen. George B. McClellan assumes command of the Federal Division of the Potomac.

friday 28 209

1861: Confederate troops occupy New Madrid, Mo., an important defensive point on the Mississippi.

saturday 29 210

1820: Clement Laird Vallandigham, leader of the Peace Democrats (Copperheads) during the Civil War, is born in New Lisbon, Ohio.

sunday 30 211

1864: Despite a huge mine explosion, Confederates fend off the second major frontal assault on Petersburg, Va.

HARRISBURG, PA., AUG. 31, 1864. My Dear Brother: . . . *All the newspaper intelligence today is cheering. I am delighted by the nomination of* [General George] McClellan [*as Democratic candidate for the US presidency*]. . . . *My boy* Oliver *has left me and enlisted. I believe he got about five hundred dollars* [*as a "bounty" for enlistment*]. *He might have got a thousand as a substitute, but he would not wait a day or two at my suggestion. Bounties seem to have gone mad. Each regiment gets about a half a million of dollars. It is all paid in new bank notes of county banks. The increase of paper circulation in this month will be fearful, probably twenty millions of dollars. We cannot carry on a war very long at this rate.* . . . *Still the* South *is much worse off, and I believe, very anxious for peace. The election of* McClellan *may change the tone of public sentiment in that region.*

—Alfred B. McCalmont, USA

AUGUST 5TH [1862, *at* Westover *plantation, 7 miles from* Baton Rouge]. . . . *About half-past nine,* . . . *a guerrilla told us the* [Confederate] *ram* Arkansas *was lying a few miles below, on her way to cooperate with* [Confederate *general*] Breckinridge, *whose advance guard had already driven the pickets into* [Union-occupied] Baton Rouge. . . . *Mother threatened us with shot and shell and bloody murder, but the loud report of half a dozen cannon in slow succession only made us more determined to see the fun.* . . . [*The carriage*] *driver, being as crazy as we, fairly made his horses run along the road to catch a glimpse of our* Ram . . . *we crossed to the outer levee, and there she lay at our feet* . . . *a heavy, clumsy, rusty, ugly flatboat with a great square box in the center, while great cannon put their noses out at the sides, and in front. The decks were crowded with men, rough and dirty, jabbering and hastily eating their breakfast. That was the great* Arkansas! God *bless and protect her, and the brave men she carries.* [*Its engines damaged and irreparable, the* Arkansas *was scuttled by its crew the next day.*]

—*Sarah Morgan*, CSA

One of the North's leading Civil War naval officers, Admiral David G. Farragut enjoyed stellar and much celebrated successes at New Orleans in 1862 and Mobile Bay in 1864. But his attempt to achieve an effective naval blockade of the Confederate Mississippi River bastion of Port Hudson in March 1863 was a failure. Located 25 miles north of Union-occupied Baton Rouge, the small town of Port Hudson was at one end of a 110-mile stretch of the Mississippi River still controlled by the Confederacy (Vicksburg was at the other). Fortified with earthworks and gun batteries well placed on the bluffs overlooking a severe bend in the river, Port Hudson was a prime—and formidably difficult—objective for Union forces. Farragut's attempt to run his entire squadron past the deadly accurate fire of Confederate guns on March 14 resulted in the loss of the USS *Mississippi* and severe damage to two other vessels. Port Hudson remained in Confederate hands until a siege and costly land assaults brought its surrender on July 9, 5 days after the fall of Vicksburg.

Admiral Farragut's Fleet Engaging the Rebel Batteries at Port Hudson, March 14th 1863
Hand-colored lithograph by Currier & Ives, c. 1863
Prints and Photographs Division
LC-USZC2-1973

s	m	t	w	t	f	s
		1	2	3	4	5
6	7	8	9	10	11	12
13	14	15	16	17	18	19
20	21	22	23	24	25	26
27	28	29	30	31		

august

1839: William Clarke Quantrill, Confederate guerrilla and outlaw, is born in Canal Dover, Ohio.

monday **31** 212

1864: Maj. Gen. Philip H. Sheridan is named commander of the Army of the Shenandoah, charged with ridding the valley of Confederates, especially Jubal Early.

tuesday **1** 213

1861: Federal Congress passes the first national income tax measure, calling for 3 percent on incomes over $800.

wednesday **2** 214

1861: A balloon ascension is made at Hampton Roads, Va., from the deck of a Federal vessel.

thursday **3** 215

1861: A meeting is held in New York to combat intemperance in the Federal army.

friday **4** 216

1864: Union forces under Adm. David Farragut defeat Confederates at the Battle of Mobile Bay.

saturday **5** 217

1811: Judah Philip Benjamin, attorney general and secretary of state of the Confederacy, is born in Saint Thomas, B.W.I.

sunday **6** 218

Appointed a US Navy midshipman at the age of 9 and a commissioned admiral—a grade especially created for him—56 years later, David Glasgow Farragut was one of the most distinguished naval figures in American history. Veteran of the War of 1812, Farragut sailed the Atlantic, the Mediterranean, and the Gulf of Mexico. At the outbreak of the Civil War, he moved his family north from their longtime base in Norfolk, Virginia. Assigned peripheral duties at first because of his Southern connections, Farragut was finally given command of the West Gulf Blockading Squadron on January 9, 1862, and proceeded to launch a daring campaign that resulted in the fall of New Orleans on April 25. His 1864 victory at the battle of Mobile Bay—where he shouted "Damn the torpedoes!" as he led his fleet past Confederate forts and the underwater mines (torpedoes) that protected them—proved the crowning event of his life.

Admiral David Glasgow Farragut (1801–1870), USA
Prints and Photographs Division
LC-B813-1561

CIVIC HOLIDAY (CANADA, MOST PROVINCES)
BANK HOLIDAY (SCOTLAND)

monday 7 219

1861: The village of Hampton, Va., near Fort Monroe, is burned by Confederate forces.

tuesday 8 220

1863: In the wake of defeat at Gettysburg, Gen. Lee offers to resign as commander of the Army of Northern Virginia. Pres. Davis rejects the offer.

wednesday 9 221

1862: Federal Army of Virginia under John Pope clashes with Stonewall Jackson's corps at the Battle of Cedar Mountain, Va.

thursday 10 222

1861: Confederate troops are victorious at the Battle of Wilson's Creek, the major battle of the Civil War in Missouri.

friday 11 223

1862: In a daring raid, Confederate guerrillas capture Independence, Mo.

saturday 12 224

1863: Pres. Lincoln refuses to give Maj. Gen. John A. McClernand, relieved of corps command at Vicksburg by Grant, a new command.

sunday 13 225

1831: Nat Turner slave insurrection begins in Southampton County, Va.; 55 whites and about 100 blacks are killed.

s	m	t	w	t	f	s
		1	2	3	4	5
6	7	8	9	10	11	12
13	14	15	16	17	18	19
20	21	22	23	24	25	26
27	28	29	30	31		

august

U. S. Tin-clad" - "St. Clair"

"U. S. Tin-clad" ~ "Argosy."

AUGUST

"... [T]he rebels mass their sharpshooters at different points and fire into our gunboats when they pass," Union naval lieutenant George Hamilton Perkins wrote in July 1863, "and although we blaze away back, we do not get a fair revenge." At the outbreak of hostilities, the United States Navy was unprepared for the sort of naval operations that the Civil War came to demand, and the Confederate navy did not exist. In the ensuing 4 years, the Confederacy built a solid naval force from scratch, and the US Navy was transformed from a skeletal force to one of the most powerful and battle-tested navies in the world. Throughout the war, naval and combined naval–land operations took place on rivers, along the Atlantic and Gulf coasts, and on the high seas. "Tin-clads," "90-day gunboats," and "Davids" (small Confederate torpedo boats that attacked larger Goliath-like ships) were among the many types of vessels employed by the North and the South. Civil War clashes of American ironclad naval vessels also signaled the beginning of a new era in naval warfare.

U.S. Tin-clad St. Clair; U.S. Tin-clad Argosy
Watercolor drawings by Ensign D. M. N. Stouffer, c. 1864–1865
David Dixon Porter Papers, Manuscript Division

s	m	t	w	t	f	s
		1	2	3	4	5
6	7	8	9	10	11	12
13	14	15	16	17	18	19
20	21	22	23	24	25	26
27	28	29	30	31		

august

monday 14 226

1861: Maj. Gen. John Charles Frémont declares martial law in St. Louis city and county.

tuesday 15 227

1864: Federals capture the English-built Confederate cruiser *Georgia* off Lisbon, Portugal.

wednesday ☾ 16 228

1862: Federal troops are defeated in an action near Lone Jack, Mo., but Confederate raiders are driven off by Northern reinforcements.

thursday 17 229

1862: Maj. Gen. James E. B. (Jeb) Stuart is assigned command of all the cavalry of the Confederate Army of Northern Virginia.

friday 18 230

1864: Battle of the Weldon Railroad, Va., begins.

saturday 19 231

1861: Confederate Congress agrees to an alliance with Missouri; Missouri now has two governments, Federal and Confederate.

sunday 20 232

1861: Maj. Gen. George B. McClellan assumes command of the Union's newly organized Department and Army of the Potomac.

Appointed a midshipman in the US Navy in 1832, John Newland Maffitt served in the West Indian Theater and in the Mediterranean before being detached to the Coast Survey, for which he spent 16 years charting the New England and South Atlantic coasts. He resigned from the US Navy in April 1861 and the next month received his commission as a lieutenant in the Confederate States Navy. During the war, he commanded a variety of transports and combat ships, including the ironclad *Albemarle* and the gunboat *Savannah.* In 1863, Maffitt was promoted to commodore after he ran a Federal blockade to reach Mobile, Alabama, in the cruiser *Florida.* The ship had not been completely equipped in Nassau, where he had taken command, and was thus unable to return the blockaders' fire. He subsequently capped that extraordinary achievement by capturing twenty-two US merchant ships. After the war, Maffitt remained at sea for a few years, sailing for the British and then for Cuban revolutionaries before settling in North Carolina, where he wrote a novel and a number of magazine articles.

Captain John Newland Maffit (1819–1886), CSN
Prints and Photographs Division
LC-USZ62-72757

s	m	t	w	t	f	s
		1	2	3	4	5
6	7	8	9	10	11	12
13	14	15	16	17	18	19
20	21	22	23	24	25	26
27	28	29	30	31		

august

monday 21 233

1863: Confederate guerrillas under Quantrill sack Lawrence, Kans., killing about 150 men and boys and destroying over $1.5 million in property.

tuesday 22 234

1862: In a raid on Catlett's Station, Va., Jeb Stuart captures Union Gen. Pope's baggage train, including the general's papers.

wednesday 23 235

1864: Fort Morgan, Mobile Bay, falls to Federals.

thursday 24 236

1862: Near the Azores, the CSS *Alabama* is commissioned by the Confederacy.

friday 25 237

1863: Following Quantrill's raid on Lawrence, Kans., Federals force some 20,000 people in Missouri from their homes, which are then burned.

saturday 26 238

1862: The Second Bull Run (or Manassas) Campaign begins.

sunday 27 239

1809: Hannibal Hamlin, US vice president under Abraham Lincoln, March 1861–March 1865, is born in Paris Hill, Maine.

CAMP AT RAPPAHANNOCK STATION, FRIDAY, SEPT. 4, 1863. My Dear Brother: . . . *My command is so small now that it seems almost ridiculous to call it a regiment, but it will become larger if we do not get into another fight.* One more battle would nearly wipe it out of existence. . . . *We get soft bread and fresh beef now all the time.* The commissary supplies are our chief dependence. *We can buy nothing in the country. It is very thinly settled in this locality, and the few people who live here are very poor. Sutlers bring us a few luxuries at fearful prices.* . . . The men have had a rough time of it. *Those of my regiment have all used more clothing than their allowance. This had been in consequence of the hard marches. They are all in debt. Troops that lay around Washington can save money on their clothing accounts. So the thing works. The harder the service the less the pay.*

—*Alfred B. McCalmont, USA*

SEPTEMBER 24TH [1862]. *Yesterday the General saluted us with "Young ladies, if you will ride in a Confederate carriage, you may go to dress parade this evening." Now in present phraseology, "Confederate" means anything that is rough, unfinished, unfashionable, or poor. You hear of Confederate dresses, which means last year's. Confederate bridle means a rope halter. Confederate silver, a tin cup or spoon . . . etc. In this case the Confederate carriage is a Jersey wagon . . . drawn by mules. We accepted gladly, partly for the ride and sight, partly to show we were not ashamed of a very comfortable conveyance. . . . And what a sad sight the Fourth Louisiana was, that was then parading! Men that had fought at Shiloh and Baton Rouge were barefooted. Rags [were their] only uniform, for very few possessed a complete suit. . . . Hats could be seen of every style and shape. . . . Yet he who had no shoes looked as happy as he who had, and he who had a cap had something to toss up, that's all.*

—*Sarah Morgan, CSA*

Told, in the summer of 1862, that the Sioux people were hungry, Minnesota trader Andrew Myrick reportedly said that "they should eat grass or their own dung." Surrounded by white people with similar attitudes, restricted to a narrow strip of land, and deprived of their hunting privileges and thus dependent on government supplies that were not being delivered, the Sioux of south-central Minnesota staged a bloody month-long uprising from mid-August to mid-September 1862—as the battles of Second Bull Run and Antietam were being fought in the east. Among the first of several hundred people to die in the uprising was Andrew Myrick as the Indians attacked both civilians and soldiers. By the end of September, the fighting had stopped and more than 1,000 Sioux were prisoners of the US Army. A military tribunal sentenced 303 of the prisoners to die by hanging and expected quick authorization for the executions from the commander-in-chief. But President Lincoln asked two lawyers to determine, by reviewing records of the trials, which of the condemned men actually led the uprising. The day after Christmas 1862, 38 of the Sioux were executed.

The Siege of New Ulm, Minn.
Reproduction of a painting by
Henry August Schwabe, 1902
Prints and Photographs Division
LC-USZC4-2995

s	m	t	w	t	f	s
					1	2
3	4	5	6	7	8	9
10	11	12	13	14	15	16
17	18	19	20	21	22	23
24	25	26	27	28	29	30

september

BANK HOLIDAY (UK EXCEPT SCOTLAND)

monday 28 240

1861: Federal forces capture Fort Hatteras, N.C., thus sealing off an important blockade-running route.

tuesday 29 241

1863: In Charleston Harbor, the Southern submersible *H. L. Hunley* sinks; five men are lost.

wednesday 30 242

1862: Second Battle of Manassas ends in defeat for the Union.

thursday 31 243

1822: Fitz-John Porter (USA) is born in Portsmouth, N.H.

friday 1 244

1864: Confederates begin evacuating Atlanta.

saturday 2 245

1864: Union forces under Gen. Sherman occupy Atlanta.

sunday 3 246

1864: In Charleston Harbor, Confederate and Union forces exchange captive surgeons and chaplains.

SEPTEMBER

A nephew of Cherokee chief Stand Watie, the only Indian to become a brigadier general in the Confederate army, Elias Cornelius Boudinot was born in the Cherokee Nation and raised in Vermont; in 1856 he settled in Arkansas, where he became a successful lawyer and politician. After serving as secretary to the Arkansas secession convention in 1861, Boudinot helped Stand Watie raise a Cherokee regiment and served briefly as its lieutenant colonel before the Cherokees elected him their representative to the Confederate Congress. He assumed office in Richmond in October 1862—after a debate on whether his election was legal under the terms of the Confederate–Cherokee treaty. Generally considered an effective advocate for the Cherokee (though his tenure was clouded by his association with an unscrupulous former Indian agent), Boudinot was appointed to the Indian Affairs Committee late in 1863 (he was allowed to introduce measures on behalf of Indians, but not to vote on them). After the war, he continued to serve as an advocate for the Cherokee.

Elias C. Boudinot (1835–1890), CSA
Prints and Photographs Division
LC-BH83-968

s	m	t	w	t	f	s
					1	2
3	4	5	6	7	8	9
10	11	12	13	14	15	16
17	18	19	20	21	22	23
24	25	26	27	28	29	30

september

LABOR DAY (US, CANADA) **monday**

1864: Famed Confederate raider and cavalry leader John Hunt Morgan is shot and killed in a Federal raid on Greeneville, Tenn. **4** 247

tuesday

1863: Under pressure from the United States, the British do not deliver two ironclads they have been building for the Confederates. **5** 248

wednesday

1819: William Starke Rosecrans (USA) is born in Delaware County, Ohio. **6** 249

thursday

1864: Gen. Sherman orders civilians in Atlanta to evacuate the city so that he might more easily feed and supply his army. ○ **7** 250

friday

1863: Confederates repulse an attack by Union gunboats and transports at Sabine Pass, on the Texas-Louisiana border. **8** 251

saturday

1863: Federal troops occupy Chattanooga, Tenn. **9** 252

sunday

1836: Joseph (Fighting Joe) Wheeler (CSA) is born in Augusta, Ga. **10** 253

SEPTEMBER

After studying law, Seneca Indian sachem Ely Samuel Parker was refused admittance to the bar on the grounds that he was not a citizen. He became instead a successful civil engineer—and an eloquent spokesman on behalf of justice for Native American peoples. Born in New York, Parker traveled to Illinois in the 1850s for engineering work and there befriended a clerk named Ulysses S. Grant. When the Civil War broke out, he returned to New York, tried for months to overcome anti-Indian prejudice and secure a military commission, and was eventually commissioned a captain. First assigned as divisional engineer under General J. E. Smith, he was soon transferred to Grant's staff and became the general-in-chief's military secretary in August 1864. Having accompanied Grant to Appomattox Court House, where the general accepted Lee's surrender, Parker was the officer who wrote down negotiated changes in the terms of capitulation when the adjutant general assigned to the task proved too nervous to write. And it was Parker who transcribed the official copies of the document that brought the war's major combat to an end.

Lieutenant Colonel Ely S. Parker (second from right), Seneca Indian chief and Ulysses S. Grant's military secretary, with General Grant's staff at City Point, Virginia, 1865
Prints and Photographs Division
LC-B811-3401

s	m	t	w	t	f	s
					1	2
3	4	5	6	7	8	9
10	11	12	13	14	15	16
17	18	19	20	21	22	23
24	25	26	27	28	29	30

september

monday 11 254

1861: Lee begins the 5-day Cheat Mountain (Va.) Campaign, which ends in a Confederate withdrawal that dims Lee's reputation for some months.

tuesday 12 255

1818: Richard Jordan Gatling, inventor of first machine gun (Gatling gun), for use in the Civil War, is born in Hertford County, N.C.

wednesday 13 256

1863: Southern cavalry seize twenty crewmen of USS *Rattler* while they attend church at Rodney, Miss.

thursday 14 257

1862: Union forces push Confederates back at the Battles of South Mountain and Crampton's Gap, Va.

friday 15 258

1862: Confederates capture Harpers Ferry, Va., taking about 12,000 prisoners.

saturday 16 259

1862: Lee gathers his forces and forms lines along Antietam Creek.

sunday 17 260

1862: Battle of Antietam halts Confederate advance into the North—the single bloodiest day of the war.

Culpepper Va Sept. 30th '63, E.F.
26

SEPTEMBER

"I don't believe we can have an army without music," said Robert E. Lee—an indication of the important roles music and musicians played in the conduct of the Civil War. In battle, cavalry and artillery were directed according to bugle signals, and infantry drummers, such as the Fourth Virginia's Private David Scantlon, became famous by risking their lives to "beat the rally," inspiring troops in the midst of combat. In camp, fifers and drummers (often the youngest men in a company) memorized drum rolls and "calls" that got the men up ("reveille"), assembled them ("second call" or the "long roll"), announced work details ("fatigue call" or "pioneer's call"), let the men know when the doctor was on duty ("surgeon's call"), and generally regulated daily life. Men who were convicted of crimes or who had exhibited cowardice in the face of the enemy were often drummed out of camp to the playing of the "rogue's march."

Drummer Boy, Taking a Rest, Culpeper, Va.
Pencil drawing by Edwin Forbes, September 30, 1863
Prints and Photographs Division
LC-USZC4-8973

s	m	t	w	t	f	s
					1	2
3	4	5	6	7	8	9
10	11	12	13	14	15	16
17	18	19	20	21	22	23
24	25	26	27	28	29	30

september

monday

1862: Lee pulls his army out of Maryland under cover of night.

18 261

tuesday

1864: Federal troops under Sheridan defeat Early's Confederates in the Third Battle of Winchester, Va.

19 262

wednesday

1863: On the second day of the Battle of Chickamauga, Confederates exploit a gap in Federal lines and cause a confused Northern retreat.

20 263

thursday

1863: Federal forces occupy a strong defensive position in and around Chattanooga, Tenn.

21 264

friday

ROSH HASHANAH (BEGINS AT SUNSET)

1862: Pres. Lincoln declares all slaves in rebellious states to be free as of January 1, 1863.

● **22** 265

saturday

AUTUMNAL EQUINOX 4:03 A.M. (GMT)

1829: George Crook (USA) is born near Dayton, Ohio.

23 266

sunday

1862: Fourteen Northern governors meet at Altoona, Pa., and approve emancipation.

24 267

CAMP AT BRISTON [SIC] STATION, VA., THURSDAY, OCT. 29, 1863. *My Dear Brother . . . It is not very easy to see the sagacity or military strategy of our recent retreat. Nor is our present advance a manifest masterstroke. . . . yet it is strange that, in spite of errors innumerable, we gain a little gradually. Still one gets sick at heart at the prospect of an interminable war. Probably the effect of all these mistakes in policy will be to make the result finally depend on the respective resources and powers of endurance of the two parties. I am not quite sure that, laying foreign interference out of the question, our true policy would not be to hold our positions in the different states, maintain the blockade and never risk a battle without almost a certainty of success. Our people at the North are very tired of the war. The army is very tired, and I presume the southern people and army are suffering far more than ours.*

—*Alfred B. McCalmont, USA*

SUNDAY, 26TH OCTOBER [1862—STAYING IN CLINTON, LOUISIANA]. *This place is completely overrun by soldiers passing and repassing. Friday night five stayed here, last night two more, and another has just gone. One, last night, a bashful Tennesseean, had never tasted sugar-cane. We were sitting around a blazing fire, enjoying it hugely, when in answer to our repeated invitations to help himself, he confessed he had never eaten it. Once instructed, though, he got on remarkably well, and ate it in a civilized manner. . . . Everything points to a speedy attack on Port Hudson. Rumors reach us from New Orleans of extensive preparations by land and water, and of the determination to burn Clinton as soon as they reach it, in revenge for the looms that were carried from Baton Rouge there, and which can soon be put in working order to supply our soldiers, negroes, and ourselves with necessary clothing.*

—*Sarah Morgan, CSA*

On November 24, 1863, encouraged by Union commander Ulysses S. Grant to show initiative as Federal forces waged their successful campaign to break the Confederate siege of Chattanooga, General Joseph Hooker led three Union divisions against Confederates holding Lookout Mountain, southwest of the city. One small Confederate division under General Carter Stevenson held the summit of the mountain, supported by troops under Edward C. Walthall and John C. Moore protecting the slopes. Fog moved in as the Federals began their assault at about 8 A.M., and it continued to inhibit both forces during the day, so that much of this "battle above the clouds" was heard but not seen by observers at Grant's headquarters. Southerners put up stiff resistance around Craven Farm, below the summit, but in the afternoon General Stevenson was ordered to withdraw from the mountain to reinforce Confederates then battling General William T. Sherman's Union forces to the northeast. All Confederate troops were successfully withdrawn by 8 P.M. By the end of the next day, the siege of Chattanooga had been broken.

Battle of Lookout Mountain
Color lithograph by Kurz & Allison, 1889
Prints and Photographs Division
LC-USZC4-1755

s	m	t	w	t	f	s
1	2	3	4	5	6	7
8	9	10	11	12	13	14
15	16	17	18	19	20	21
22	23	24	25	26	27	28
29	30	31				

october

monday 25 268

1864: Union troops under Sheridan force Jubal Early's Confederates to retreat before them as they advance toward Staunton and Waynesborough, Va.

tuesday 26 269

1863: Pres. Lincoln and others are distressed when the *New York Post* reveals the movement of reinforcements to Chattanooga.

wednesday 27 270

1809: Raphael Semmes, Confederate naval commander responsible for destruction or capture of 64 Union ships, is born in Charles County, Md.

thursday 28 271

1863: Federal Gens. Alexander McCook and T. L. Crittenden are relieved of their commands and ordered to a court of inquiry re the Battle of Chickamauga.

friday 29 272

1862: Federal Brig. Gen. Jefferson Davis shoots and mortally wounds Brig. Gen. William "Bull" Nelson during a quarrel in a hotel in Louisville.

saturday 30 273

1864: Lee unsuccessfully counterattacks Fort Harrison, Va., lost to the Union the day before.

sunday 1 274

YOM KIPPUR (BEGINS AT SUNSET)

1864: Famed Confederate spy Mrs. Rose O'Neal Greenhow drowns as she tries to avoid capture.

2426

OCTOBER

"Grant is my man," President Lincoln said, after Grant's forces took Vicksburg, Mississippi, "and I am his for the rest of the war." Grant followed his Vicksburg triumph by breaking the Confederate siege of Chattanooga and was shortly summoned to Washington to receive command of all Union armies. The Chattanooga victory also inspired an admirer in St. Louis to give Grant a magnificent and aristocratic horse, which would become his most famous charger. Standing tall at seventeen and a half hands, Cincinnati was the son of Lexington, a champion thoroughbred. Grant, an exceptional horseman, had several other mounts—including a comparatively small horse named Jeff Davis that his men had liberated from the plantation of the Confederate president's brother—but Cincinnati quickly became his favorite. He would not allow anyone else to ride the huge charger, with one exception. President Lincoln, whom Grant considered an excellent horseman, was permitted to ride Cincinnati whenever the commander-in-chief visited Grant at the front.

Ulysses S. Grant and his war horse Cincinnati
Photograph by Jarvis at Cold Harbor, Virginia, June 4, 1864
Prints and Photographs Division
LC-USZC4-4579

s	m	t	w	t	f	s
1	2	3	4	5	6	7
8	9	10	11	12	13	14
15	16	17	18	19	20	21
22	23	24	25	26	27	28
29	30	31				

october

1800: Nat Turner, slave, leader of insurrection at Southampton, Va., is born in Southampton County.

monday 2 275

1863: Federal war department orders enlistment of Negro troops in the slave states of Maryland, Missouri, and Tennessee.

tuesday 3 276

1862: Battle of Corinth, Miss., ends with a Confederate withdrawal from this important rail and road center.

wednesday 4 277

1863: Confederate torpedo boat *David*, with a four-man crew, attacks Federal ironclad *New Ironsides* outside Charleston Harbor.

thursday 5 278

1861: Confederate blockade runner *Alert* is captured by the Federal navy off Charleston, S.C.

friday 6 279

1864: USS *Wachusett* captures the troublesome raider CSS *Florida* in a controversial action at Bahia, Brazil.

saturday ○ 7 280

1861: Brig. Gen. William T. Sherman is named to command the Union Department of the Cumberland, with headquarters at Louisville.

sunday 8 281

OCTOBER

A West Point graduate with combat experience against the Seminoles in Florida and in the Mexican War, Braxton Bragg was an energetic but quarrelsome officer who had trouble securing the loyalty of his subordinates. Retired from the US Army in 1856, he was a Louisiana plantation owner and commissioner of public works until the secession movement began. First joining the Louisiana militia, Bragg was soon commissioned a brigadier general in the Confederate States Army and assigned to command the coast between Pensacola and Mobile. After promotion to major general, he became a corps commander and chief of staff under A. S. Johnston, fought well at Shiloh, and eventually was given command of the Army of Tennessee. Although he won notable victories at Stone's River, Tennessee, and Chickamauga, Bragg did not follow up on his successes. After his defeat at Chattanooga in November 1863, he surrendered his command to Joseph Johnston. He finished the war as a military adviser to President Davis and in several minor commands, fighting his last battle on March 8, 1865, in North Carolina.

General Braxton Bragg (1817–1876), CSA
Prints and Photographs Division
LC-USZ62-4888

s	m	t	w	t	f	s
1	2	3	4	5	6	7
8	9	10	11	12	13	14
15	16	17	18	19	20	21
22	23	24	25	26	27	28
29	30	31				

october

COLUMBUS DAY OBSERVED — monday
THANKSGIVING DAY (CANADA)
9 282

1864: Union cavalry under George Custer and Wesley Merritt engage and rout Confederates at Tom's Brook (Round Top Mountain), Va.

tuesday **10** 283

1862: Pres. Davis asks Virginia for a draft of 4,500 Negroes to work on completion of fortifications of Richmond.

wednesday **11** 284

1861: Brig. Gen. William S. Rosecrans assumes command of the Federal Department of Western Virginia.

COLUMBUS DAY — thursday **12** 285

1861: First ironclad of the Union navy, the gunboat *St. Louis,* is launched at Carondelet, Mo.

friday **13** 286

1864: Maryland voters narrowly adopt a new state constitution abolishing slavery.

saturday ☾ **14** 287

1863: Confederates strike retreating Federals at Bristoe Station, Va., in an inconclusive engagement.

sunday **15** 288

1863: In Charleston Harbor, Confederate submersible *H. L. Hunley* sinks for a second time during a practice dive. Seven men, including Hunley, the inventor, die.

OCTOBER

A prominent and capable lawyer, Edwin Stanton served briefly as attorney general under President Buchanan before his appointment as US secretary of war in January 1862. He proceeded to reform this crucial department, which had been subject to graft and corruption, and ran it with a grim efficiency dedicated to aggressive prosecution of the war. Stanton's pre-war friendship with General George McClellan ended as he grew impatient with the general's inactivity; other officers and civilians also earned the ire of this able but contentious man. Even those angered, however, did not question Stanton's capacities or his devotion to supporting the troops in the field. One of his greatest wartime achievements was the dispatch of reinforcements to relieve the Union troops besieged by Confederates in Chattanooga. Organized under the press of potential disaster, this emergency relief—20,000 soldiers of the Army of the Potomac and their equipment, horses, and artillery—was assembled, loaded, transported, and safely conveyed the 1,200 miles to Tennessee within 11 days.

Secretary of War Edwin M. Stanton (1814–1869), USA
Photograph by the Brady National Photographic Art Gallery
Prints and Photographs Division
LC-B8172-2208

s	m	t	w	t	f	s
1	2	3	4	5	6	7
8	9	10	11	12	13	14
15	16	17	18	19	20	21
22	23	24	25	26	27	28
29	30	31				

october

monday 16 289

1859: John Brown, US abolitionist, leads an unsuccessful raid on the government arsenal at Harpers Ferry, Va.

tuesday 17 290

1863: Pres. Lincoln issues a proclamation calling for 300,000 more volunteers for Federal armies.

wednesday 18 291

1862: John Hunt Morgan and his Confederate raiders defeat Federal cavalry near Lexington, Ky.

thursday 19 292

1864: A small Confederate raiding party robs three Vermont banks of over $200,000.

friday 20 293

1864: Pres. Lincoln proclaims the last Thursday in November "a day of Thanksgiving and Praise to Almighty God. . . ."

saturday 21 294

1861: Federal forces suffer a dramatic, costly defeat at the Battle of Ball's Bluff (Leesburg), Va.

sunday 22 295

1862: Confederate cavalry take London, Ky.

OCTOBER

Among the first people to be regarded as a "war correspondent," William Howard Russell was dispatched to the United States in February 1861 by the *London Times* "to act as the Special Correspondent of that paper in observing the rupture between the Southern States and the rest of the Union. . . ." Famous for his reports of the Crimean War, Russell had easy access to politicians and military commanders. His dispatches to the paper were followed by a book, *My Diary North and South*—published in 1863 and republished several times—filled with this acute but sometimes jaded outsider's observations in the midst of conflict-torn America. "A public man in the United States is very much like a great firework," he wrote in October 1861; "he commences with some small scintillations which attract the eye of the public, and then he blazes up and flares out in blue, purple, and orange fires, to the intense admiration of the multitude, and dying out suddenly is thought of no more, his place being taken by a fresh Roman candle or catherine wheel which is thought to be far finer. . . ."

Sir William Howard Russell (1820–1907), war correspondent
Brady-Handy Collection,
Prints and Photographs Division
LC-BH82-5087B

s	m	t	w	t	f	s
1	2	3	4	5	6	7
8	9	10	11	12	13	14
15	16	17	18	19	20	21
22	23	24	25	26	27	28
29	30	31				

october

monday 23 296

1864: Last Confederate effort in Missouri ends in defeat at the Battle of Westport, Mo.

tuesday 24 297

UNITED NATIONS DAY

1861: Western Union completes the first transcontinental telegraph.

wednesday 25 298

1861: The keel of the ironclad USS *Monitor* is laid at Greenpoint, Long Island.

thursday 26 299

1864: Confederate guerrilla Bloody Bill Anderson is killed in an ambush near Richmond, Mo.

friday 27 300

1864: In a daring adventure, Union Lt. William B. Cushing and a fifteen-man crew sink the Confederate ironclad *Albemarle* at Plymouth, N.C.

saturday 28 301

1862: Confederate Maj. Gen. John C. Breckinridge assumes command of the Army of Middle Tennessee.

sunday 29 302

DAYLIGHT SAVING TIME ENDS

SUMMER TIME ENDS (UK)

1861: Largest combined land-sea expedition ever mounted by the United States leaves Hampton Roads, Va., for the Carolina coast and Port Royal.

CAMP, NEAR AQUIA CREEK, SATURDAY, NOV. 22, 1862. *My Dear Brother . . . The march today . . . lay through a miserable looking country, covered with dwarf pine trees and here and there marked by the ruins of some old plantation, from which fences and houses have disappeared. . . . The soldiers marched through the woods, following a blazed track not far from a poor country road. . . . We occasionally crossed the road, over which by the aid of corduroy improvements, the ambulances, buggies, wagons and artillery were making slow and tedious progress. We could hear the drivers whipping and swearing, and sometimes see a wagon stuck fast in the mud. On the way a boy met us with the "Philadelphia Inquirer," and there was a great deal of laughing over one of the headings of army news which pithily stated in substance, but in large capitals, that the army's advance was not impeded by the rain.*

–Alfred B. McCalmont, USA

MONDAY, NOVEMBER 30TH [1863]. *Our distress about Gibbes [Sarah's brother, now a prisoner of war] has been somewhat relieved by good news from Jimmy [another brother, serving in the Confederate navy]. The jolliest sailor letter from him . . . detailing his cruise on the Georgia [a commerce raider]. . . . What a jolly life it must be! Now dashing in storms and danger, now floating in sunshine and fun! . . . Then how he changes, in describing the prize [a US vessel] with an assorted cargo that they took, which contained all things from a needle to pianos, from the reckless spurt in which he speaks of the plundering, to where he tells of how the Captain, having died several days before, was brought on the Georgia while [the Georgia's captain, Commander W. L.] Maury read the service over the body and consigned it to the deep by the flames of the dead man's own vessel. What noble, tender, manly hearts it shows, those rough seamen stopping in the work of destruction to perform the last rites over their dead enemy.*

–Sarah Morgan, CSA

OCT/NOV

[April 15, 1865] The news of Lee's surrender is true. Better than all my hopes was the prospect of the end of the war. . . . Joy on every face and tongue. I could not see or hear of a secession sympathizer. . . . I went to bed happy, thinking of the glorious change, and came down this morning to be astounded by the news that President Lincoln was assassinated last night at Ford's Theater in Washington and Secretary [of State] Seward and his son were stabbed at almost the same hour. . . . It is too terrible to think of, and I cannot imagine the consequences. . . . What can we do with such a President as Andy Johnson? What effect will it have on the question of peace? Well, we can do nothing but wait. The nation's joy is changed to mourning and to mutterings of vengeance on the cowardly assassins and the infamous plotters who arranged the murders.

[May 7, 1865] . . . Well, we may say the war is over—"this cruel war is over." The joy of the nation is tempered by its grief at the base assassination of the President, but we can console ourselves by the thought that he had accomplished his work.
—Lieutenant Oliver Willcox Norton, USA, letters to his brother and sister

Funeral car of President Lincoln, New York, April 26th, 1865
Watercolor drawing by P. Relyea, 1879
Prints and Photographs Division
LC-USZC4-2337

s	m	t	w	t	f	s
			1	2	3	4
5	6	7	8	9	10	11
12	13	14	15	16	17	18
19	20	21	22	23	24	25
26	27	28	29	30		

november

monday 30 303

1863: Unconditional unionists of Arkansas meet at Fort Smith, naming a representative to Congress.

tuesday 31 304

HALLOWEEN

1864: Nevada becomes the 36th state in the Union.

wednesday 1 305

1861: Maj. Gen. George B. McClellan succeeds retiring Lt. Gen. Winfield Scott as general-in-chief of the Union armies.

thursday 2 306

1861: Maj. Gen. John C. Frémont is relieved of command of the Union's Western Department.

friday 3 307

1816: Jubal Anderson Early (CSA) is born in Franklin County, Va.

saturday 4 308

1862: With conquest of Vicksburg in mind, Gen. Grant's forces occupy La Grange and Grand Junction, Tenn.

sunday 5 309

1818: Soldier-politician Benjamin Franklin Butler (USA) is born in Deerfield, N.H.

1862: Pres. Lincoln relieves McClellan of command of the Army of the Potomac, replacing him with Burnside.

NOVEMBER

It is not merely for today, but for all time to come that we should perpetuate for our children's children this great and free government, which we have enjoyed all our lives. I beg you to remember this, not merely for my sake, but for yours. I happen temporarily to occupy this big White House. I am a living witness that any one of your children may look to come here as my father's child has. It is in order that each of you may have through this free government which we have enjoyed, an open field and a fair chance for your industry, enterprise and intelligence; that you may all have equal privileges in the race of life, with all its desirable human aspirations. It is for this the struggle should be maintained, that we may not lose our birthright. . . . The nation is worth fighting for, to secure such an inestimable jewel.

—Abraham Lincoln, address to the 166th Ohio regiment, August 22, 1864

Abraham Lincoln looking at an album with his son Tad

Arthur Wallace Dunn Papers,
Prints and Photographs Division
LC-USZ62-92539

s	m	t	w	t	f	s
			1	2	3	4
5	6	7	8	9	10	11
12	13	14	15	16	17	18
19	20	21	22	23	24	25
26	27	28	29	30		

november

1860: Abraham Lincoln is elected president of the United States.

monday

6 310

ELECTION DAY

tuesday

1837: Elijah Parish Lovejoy (b. 1802), US abolitionist and newspaperman, is killed in a riot over the slavery issue; he becomes known as the "martyr abolitionist."

7 311

1864: Abraham Lincoln is reelected president of the United States, with Andrew Johnson of Tennessee as vice president.

wednesday

8 312

1825: A. P. (Ambrose Powell) Hill (CSA) is born in Culpeper, Va.

thursday

9 313

VETERANS DAY OBSERVED

friday

1862: Maj. Gen. McClellan takes an emotional, spectacular farewell of the Army of the Potomac.

10 314

VETERANS DAY

REMEMBRANCE DAY (CANADA)

saturday

1864: Federals at Rome, Ga., destroy bridges, foundries, warehouses, and other property of use to the enemy and proceed toward Atlanta.

11 315

1861: The Confederate blockade runner *Fingal*, bought in England, arrives in Savannah with military supplies.

sunday

12 316

W.O.B. Branch
Earl Van Dorn
J.H. Morgan
W. Barksdale
A.S. Johnston
J.E.B. Stuart
"Stonewall" Jackson
J.S. Bowen
Zollicoffer
L. Tilghman
A.J. Jenkins
Ben. Mc. Cullough
Leonidas Polk
G.J. Rains
Confederate Dead

NOVEMBER

The huge armies that both sides had mustered began returning home not long after Lee's surrender at Appomattox Court House. On April 24, 1865, David Lane, a proud Union soldier who was impatient to be a civilian again, wrote in his journal as he arrived at Alexandria, Virginia: "One year ago we passed through this city on our way to Richmond. Today we tread its streets with buoyant feet, . . . our work accomplished. . . . 'Tis a long, weary road, the one we traveled, but what matter now? . . . We are going home." Men of the former Confederate States, now a devastated land, saw the end of the fighting through very different eyes: "I am as one walking in a dream, & expecting to awake," former Confederate chief of ordnance Josiah Gorgas wrote in his diary on May 4. ". . . It is marvelous that a people that a month ago had money, armies, and the attributes of a nation should today be no more, & that we live, breathe, move, talk as before." Fully a quarter of the South's military-age white men did not return home. North and South, some 620,000 people had perished in the war.

Confederate dead: memorial photographs of Earl Van Dorn, John H. Morgan, William Barksdale, Albert Sidney Johnston, Jeb Stuart, Stonewall Jackson, J. S. Bowen, Felix Zollicoffer, Lloyd Tilghman, Albert Gallatin Jenkins, Ben McCollough, Leonidas Polk, and G. J. Rains
Prints and Photographs Division
LC-B813-6793

s	m	t	w	t	f	s
			1	2	3	4
5	6	7	8	9	10	11
12	13	14	15	16	17	18
19	20	21	22	23	24	25
26	27	28	29	30		

november

1814: Joseph ("Fighting Joe") Hooker (USA) is born in Hadley, Mass.

monday **13** 317

1862: In New Orleans, a proclamation calls for election of members of the US Congress from portions of the state held by Federals.

tuesday **14** 318

1861: The YMCA organizes the US Christian Commission for service to Federal soldiers.

wednesday **15** 319

1864: Gen. Sherman and 60,000 Union troops leave a burned-out Atlanta, beginning their famous March to the Sea.

thursday **16** 320

1863: Confederate siege of Knoxville, Tenn., gets under way; partial siege of Chattanooga continues.

friday **17** 321

1864: Pres. Davis tells Gen. Howell Cobb at Macon to "get out every man who can render any service even for a short period" to oppose Sherman.

saturday **18** 322

1863: Abraham Lincoln delivers the Gettysburg Address at the dedication ceremony for a new national cemetery.

sunday **19** 323

NOVEMBER

Born into a wealthy and influential Kentucky family, Mary Todd moved, in 1839, into her sister's household in Springfield, Illinois; shortly thereafter, she met a lawyer named Lincoln (also Kentucky born), whom she married in 1842. Five feet 2 inches tall to his 6 feet 4, stubborn, willful, and often sarcastic, Mrs. Lincoln embarked on 23 years of marriage marked by mutual love (as well as some mutual frustration) and marred by multiple tragedies—including the deaths of two of the Lincolns' four sons (their youngest son, Tad, was to die in 1871). As US First Lady, Mrs. Lincoln was scorned as a traitor by Southerners (though her native state of Kentucky had remained in the Union, the Confederacy also claimed the state). At the same time, many in the North suspected her, unfairly, of being sympathetic to the South. Like many Americans, Mrs. Lincoln had loved ones on both sides. Married to the Union commander-in-chief, she was also sister-in-law to Confederate general Benjamin H. Helm and half-sister of three Confederate soldiers, Aleck, Sam, and David Todd—all of whom died of war wounds.

Mrs. Abraham (Mary Todd) Lincoln (1818–1882), USA
Brady-Handy Collection,
Prints and Photographs Division
LC-BH824-4575

s	m	t	w	t	f	s
			1	2	3	4
5	6	7	8	9	10	11
12	13	14	15	16	17	18
19	20	21	22	23	24	25
26	27	28	29	30		

november

monday 20 324

1862: Gen. Lee arrives at Fredericksburg, Va., as buildup of Union and Confederate troops continues on the Rappahannock.

tuesday 21 325

1861: Pres. Davis names Judah P. Benjamin secretary of war.

1862: Pres. Davis appoints James A. Seddon secretary of war.

wednesday 22 326

1864: Gen. Slocum's wing of Sherman's army occupies Georgia state capital at Milledgeville.

thursday 23 327

THANKSGIVING DAY

1803: Theodore Dwight Weld, "the Great Abolitionist," is born in Hampton, Conn.

friday 24 328

1862: Confederate Gen. Joseph E. Johnston is assigned to the major command in the West, comprising six states.

saturday 25 329

1864: Confederate agents set fires in ten or more New York hotels and in Barnum's Museum; none does serious damage.

sunday 26 330

1861: A convention at Wheeling adopts a constitution for a new state to be called West Virginia, created by secession from Virginia.

CAMP AT AVERY HOUSE, VA., DEC. 16, 1864. *My Dear Brother: We have had quite an exciting afternoon. The enemy opened on us with a battery that we had not previously heard from. They seemed to have a particular design on our camp. . . . Our batteries took the matter in hand and opened with spirit, and there was a heavy cannonading kept up from two o-clock till sundown. . . . All is now quiet, but the firing of pickets which is generally kept up without interruption all night long. This state of things has become chronic. . . . We have an official announcement of another victory by [Union general George H.] Thomas, also rumors that Savannah has been captured by Sherman, and that the negro troops have taken the Howlett Battery, a formidable fort, which is on the left of the Confederate defenses at Bermuda Hundred. I hope that one and all of these items of good news will prove to be true. . . .*

—Alfred B. McCalmont, USA

THURSDAY NIGHT, DECEMBER 31ST, 1863. *The last of 1863 is passing away as I write. . . . Every New Year since I was in my teens, I have sought a quiet spot where I could whisper to myself Tennyson's "Death of the Old Year," and even this bitter cold night I steal into my freezing, fireless little room, . . . to keep up my old habit while the others sleep. . . .*

OLD YEAR, YOU SHALL NOT DIE;
WE DID SO LAUGH AND CRY WITH YOU,
I'VE HALF A MIND TO DIE WITH YOU,
OLD YEAR, IF YOU MUST DIE.

No! Go and welcome! Bring Peace and brighter days, O dawning New Year. Die, faster and faster, Old One; I count your remaining moments with almost savage glee.

—*Sarah Morgan, CSA*

NOV/DEC

The Civil War was America's costliest and most rending conflict, a contest of unprecedented violence that was led, in many instances, by men who had once been comrades in arms, congressional colleagues, and friends. While serving in the US Congress, Jefferson Davis, for example, forged a friendship with Senator William H. Seward that endured despite Seward's adamant Unionism and stalwart service as Abraham Lincoln's secretary of state. Leading generals of both sides attended West Point together and fought side by side on the frontiers and in the Mexican War. Sometimes, as with George B. Crittenden (general, CSA) and Thomas L. Crittenden (general, USA), they were brothers. Sharing pride in America's Revolutionary heritage, most leaders of both sides, as well as the people they led, believed deeply in the principles expressed in the founding documents of the United States, but they grew to interpret these principles differently. The two fundamental differences—regarding slavery and the primacy of the Union over individual states—were resolved by the conflict.

Prominent Union and Confederate Generals and Statesmen as They Appeared During the Great Civil War, 1861–5
Color lithograph by Kurz & Allison, 1885
Prints and Photographs Division
LC-USZC4-1734

s	m	t	w	t	f	s
					1	2
3	4	5	6	7	8	9
10	11	12	13	14	15	16
17	18	19	20	21	22	23
24	25	26	27	28	29	30
31						

december

monday 27 331

1863: Gen. John Hunt Morgan and several of his officers escape from the Ohio State Penitentiary and manage to reach Confederate territory.

tuesday 28 332

1861: Southern Congress officially admits Missouri to the Confederate States of America.

wednesday 29 333

1864: Federal army under John Schofield withdraws under Hood's nose without suffering attack in the "Spring Hill [Tenn.] Affair."

thursday 30 334

1863: Gathering his defeated army in northwest Georgia, Braxton Bragg learns that his resignation has been accepted by Jefferson Davis.

friday 1 335

1861: US gunboat *Penguin* captures the blockade runner *Albion* of Nassau off Charleston and confiscates her cargo.

saturday 2 336

1863: Gen. Braxton Bragg turns over command of the Army of Tennessee to Lt. Gen. William Hardee at Dalton, Ga.

sunday 3 337

1826: George Brinton McClellan (USA) is born in Philadelphia.

To all whom it may Concern:

Know ye, That ....
.... of ....
Company (......) .... Regiment of ....
VOLUNTEERS who was enrolled on the .... day of ....
one thousand eight hundred and .... to serve .... years
or during the war, is hereby Discharged from the service of the
United States, this .... day of .... 186 , at
.... by reason of ....
(No objection to his being re-enlisted is known to exist.)*
Said .... was born in ....
in the State of ...., is .... years of age
.... feet .... inches high .... complexion, ... eyes
.... hair, and by occupation, when enrolled, a ....
Given at .... this .... day of
.... 18 ....

* This sentence will be erased should there be anything in the conduct or physical condition of the Soldier rendering unfit for the Army.

PUBLISHED BY CURRIER & IVES, Entered according to Act of Congress AD 1865, by Currier & Ives, in the Clerk's Office of the District Court of the United States, for the Southern ... N.Y. 152 NASSAU ST. NEW YORK.

THE UNION SOLDIER'S DISCHARGE CERTIFICATE.

May 21st, 1865: The long-delayed, eagerly-looked-for order has been issued; read to us on dress parade. "All troops whose term of service expires on or before the first day of October, 1865, shall be mustered out immediately." and our officers are to make out their final muster-out rolls without delay. Recruits are to be transferred to veteran regiments, which will be retained for a time. . . .

May 31st, 1865
Dearest Wife:
It is useless for you to write to me again, darling, and this is the last letter you will get from your soldier. Before this reaches you, I will be on my homeward way, a full-fledged citizen, and as I come, my glad heart will sing the joyous refrain: "Oh, I come, I come, ye have called me long; I come o'er the mountain with light and song."
Yours lovingly.
David Lane, USA

The Union Soldier's Discharge Certificate
Lithograph by Currier & Ives, 1865
Prints and Photographs Division
LC-USZ62-104551

s	m	t	w	t	f	s
					1	2
3	4	5	6	7	8	9
10	11	12	13	14	15	16
17	18	19	20	21	22	23
24	25	26	27	28	29	30
31						

december

monday 4 338

1862: Confederate Gen. Joseph E. Johnston assumes overall command in the West.

tuesday 5 339

1839: George Armstrong Custer (USA) is born in New Rumley, Ohio.

wednesday 6 340

1833: John Singleton Mosby (CSA) is born in Edgemont, Va.
1864: Pres. Lincoln reports that in the year ending July 1, 1863, the War and Navy Departments had spent $776,525,135.74.

thursday 7 341

1862: Confederate raider John Hunt Morgan, with 1,400 men, surprises a Federal garrison at Hartsville, Tenn., taking 1,800 prisoners.

friday 8 342

1862: Pres. Lincoln issues Proclamation of Amnesty and Reconstruction, pardoning participants "in the existing rebellion" if they take an oath to the Union.

saturday 9 343

1863: Negro Federal troops at Fort Jackson, La., mutiny over alleged mistreatment by one white officer of his soldiers.

sunday 10 344

1861: An act of the Confederate Congress in Richmond admits Kentucky to the Confederacy, thus completing the thirteen states.

DECEMBER

The site of the war's beginning, when Major Robert Anderson's small US garrison was besieged and finally fired upon by Confederate forces in April 1861, Fort Sumter, in Charleston, South Carolina's harbor, became a focal point for Union action in 1863, when a new Federal campaign was initiated by a squadron of nine Union ironclads. Charleston and its defenses remained a prime target of Union bombardments until the city and its fortifications were evacuated by Confederates on February 17, 1865. On April 14, precisely 4 years after he had surrendered the fort, Anderson, now a general, participated in a happier Fort Sumter ceremony, hoisting the same flag he had been forced to lower in 1861 over the reclaimed bastion before a gathering of Northern officers and dignitaries. Henry Ward Beecher, brother of Harriet Beecher Stowe, delivered a speech, and the solemn but joyful ceremonies continued into the evening. As they were concluding with fireworks, President Lincoln, in Washington, was preparing to go to Ford's Theater to see a performance of the comedy *Our American Cousin.*

Charleston, South Carolina: Fort Sumter from the Sand-bar
Photograph by George N. Barnard, April 1865
Prints and Photographs Division
LC-B8171-3047

s	m	t	w	t	f	s
					1	2
3	4	5	6	7	8	9
10	11	12	13	14	15	16
17	18	19	20	21	22	23
24	25	26	27	28	29	30
31						

december

monday **11** 345

1861: Already suffering under the Federal blockade, Charleston, S.C., is struck by a disastrous fire that sweeps through its business district.

tuesday **12** 346

1862: On the Yazoo River, Miss., the Federal ironclad *Cairo* strikes a mine and sinks; the crew escapes.

wednesday **13** 347

1818: Mary Todd Lincoln, wife of Abraham Lincoln, is born in Lexington, Ky.

thursday **14** 348

1861: Brig. Gen. H. H. Sibley assumes command of the Confederate forces on the upper Rio Grande and in New Mexico and Arizona Territories.

friday **15** 349

HANUKKAH (BEGINS AT SUNSET)

1863: Confederate Maj. Gen. Jubal A. Early is assigned to the Shenandoah Valley District.

saturday **16** 350

1864: Battle of Nashville ends as a Confederate army commanded by Gen. John B. Hood is almost destroyed by Union troops under Gen. George H. Thomas.

sunday **17** 351

1861: Federals sink several old hulks loaded with stones in Savannah Harbor in an effort to halt shipping.

DECEMBER

Among the most dedicated and talented, and undoubtedly the most prolific, of the Civil War special artists, "Alf" Waud (pronounced Wode) helped convey battlefield action and the feel of camp life to home audiences—and to people of future generations—with an immediacy the cumbersome photographic processes of the period could not achieve (Civil War "action photographs" were technologically impossible). The life of these artists, as described by one of Waud's colleagues, Theodore Davis, involved "total disregard for personal safety and comfort; an owl-like propensity to sit up all night and a hawky style of vigilance during the day; . . . willingness to ride any number of miles horseback for just one sketch, which might have to be finished at night by no better light than that of a fire." Waud and Davis were the only two special artists to work continuously throughout the war, and Waud continued to report on the effects of the conflict. After the fighting stopped, he made an extended tour of the Southern states. Many of the resulting sketches were published in *Harper's Weekly.*

Special artist Alfred R. Waud (1828–1891), USA
Prints and Photographs Division
LC-USZ62-533

s	m	t	w	t	f	s
					1	2
3	4	5	6	7	8	9
10	11	12	13	14	15	16
17	18	19	20	21	22	23
24	25	26	27	28	29	30
31						

december

monday 18 352

1865: Thirteenth Amendment to the US Constitution abolishing slavery is declared in effect by Secretary of State Seward after approval by twenty-seven states.

tuesday 19 353

1814: Edwin McMasters Stanton, US secretary of war 1862–1869, is born in Steubenville, Ohio.

wednesday 20 354

1860: In Charleston, the South Carolina Convention passes a formal declaration of secession (first state to secede).

thursday 21 355

1864: Gen. Sherman and his Union army enter Savannah, Ga., with no opposition.

friday 22 356

WINTER SOLSTICE 12:22 A.M. (GMT)

1864: Gen. Sherman sends Pres. Lincoln a message: "I beg to present you, as a Christmas gift, the city of Savannah. . . ."

saturday 23 357

1864: A Federal fleet rendezvouses near Wilmington, N.C., for an attack on Fort Fisher.

sunday 24 358

1864: A Federal fleet bombards Fort Fisher, N.C., which guards Wilmington, the last open Confederate port.

BANKING OFFICE

DECEMBER

On February 18, 1865, the 21st US Colored Troops and two companies of the 54th Massachusetts were among the first Union troops to enter Charleston, South Carolina, the city where the war began. Fighting on two fronts, the Union's black soldiers had helped win signal victories on both: Southern armies were defeated and, with ratification of the Thirteenth Amendment in December 1865, slavery in the United States was at an end. Yet when the Army of the Potomac and William T. Sherman's western armies marched through the heart of Washington, DC, in a spectacular Grand Review on May 23–24, 1865, the only African Americans among the marchers were contrabands walking with Sherman's troops. Not one of the 166 regiments of US Colored Troops was included in this celebration. The Reconstruction era would witness reverses to the progress black soldiers had helped African Americans achieve during the Civil War. America's black soldiers would be required to fight on two fronts in future wars well into the twentieth century, having to win, again and again, recognition as able and devoted citizen soldiers.

Negro Soldiers Mustered Out
Pencil and Chinese white drawing on green paper by Alfred Waud, 1866
Prints and Photographs Division
LC-USZC4-2042

s	m	t	w	t	f	s
					1	2
3	4	5	6	7	8	9
10	11	12	13	14	15	16
17	18	19	20	21	22	23
24	25	26	27	28	29	30
31						

december

CHRISTMAS DAY

monday 25 359

1864: Federals land troops to take Fort Fisher, N.C., but the assault fails and they are withdrawn.

KWANZAA BEGINS
BOXING DAY (CANADA, UK)

tuesday 26 360

1862: Federals attack a guerrilla camp in Powell County, Ky.

wednesday 27 361

1860: The US flag is raised over Fort Sumter as South Carolina troops occupy Charleston forts.

thursday 28 362

1862: Federal Army of the Frontier pushes back Confederates at Dripping Springs, Ark., capturing Van Buren, Ark.

friday 29 363

1808: Andrew Johnson, 17th US president (1865–1869), succeeding Abraham Lincoln, is born in Raleigh, N.C.

saturday 30 364

1862: USS *Monitor,* hero of the battle with the *Merrimack,* founders off Cape Hatteras in heavy seas; sixteen officers and men are lost.

sunday 31 365

1815: George Gordon Meade (USA) is born in Cadiz, Spain.

2006 INTERNATIONAL HOLIDAYS

Following are major (bank-closing) holidays for selected countries in 2006. Islamic observances are subject to adjustment. Holidays for the US, UK, and Canada and major Jewish holidays appear on this calendar's grid pages. Pomegranate is not responsible for errors or omissions in this list. Users of this information should confirm dates with local sources before making international travel or business plans.

Argentina

1 Jan	New Year's Day
3 Apr	Malvinas Islands Memorial
13 Apr	Holy Thursday
14 Apr	Good Friday
16 Apr	Easter
1 May	Labor Day
25 May	Revolution of May 1810
19 Jun	Flag Day
9 Jul	Independence Day
21 Aug	General San Martín Anniversary
16 Oct	Columbus Day
8 Dec	Immaculate Conception
25 Dec	Christmas

Australia

1–2 Jan	New Year's Holiday
26 Jan	Australia Day
6 Mar	Labor Day (WA)
13 Mar	Labor Day (Vic)
	Eight Hours Day (Tas)
14 Apr	Good Friday
15 Apr	Easter Saturday (NSW)
16–17 Apr	Easter Holiday
25 Apr	Anzac Day
1 May	Labor Day (Qld)
12 Jun	Queen's Birthday
7 Aug	Bank Holiday (NSW, NT)
2 Oct	Labor Day (NSW, ACT, SA)
7 Nov	Melbourne Cup Day (Vic)
25 Dec	Christmas
26 Dec	Boxing Day

Brazil

1 Jan	New Year's Day
20 Jan	São Sebastião Day (Rio de Janeiro)
25 Jan	São Paulo Anniversary (São Paulo)
27–28 Feb	Carnival
14 Apr	Good Friday
16 Apr	Easter
21 Apr	Tiradentes Day
1 May	Labor Day
15 Jun	Corpus Christi
9 Jul	State Holiday (São Paulo)
7 Sep	Independence Day
12 Oct	Our Lady of Aparecida
2 Nov	All Souls' Day
15 Nov	Proclamation of the Republic
20 Nov	Zumbi dos Palmares Day (Rio de Janeiro)
25 Dec	Christmas

China (see also Hong Kong)

1–2 Jan	New Year's Holiday
29–31 Jan	Lunar New Year
1–3 May	Labor Day Holiday
1–3 Oct	National Holiday

France

1 Jan	New Year's Day
14 Apr	Good Friday
16–17 Apr	Easter Holiday
1 May	Labor Day
8 May	Armistice Day (WWII)
25 May	Ascension Day
5 Jun	Whitmonday
14 Jul	Bastille Day
15 Aug	Assumption Day
1 Nov	All Saints' Day
11 Nov	Armistice Day (WWI)
25 Dec	Christmas

Germany

1 Jan	New Year's Day
6 Jan	Epiphany (Munich)
14 Apr	Good Friday
16–17 Apr	Easter Holiday
1 May	Labor Day
25 May	Ascension Day
5 Jun	Whitmonday
15 Jun	Corpus Christi
15 Aug	Assumption Day (Munich)
3 Oct	Unity Day
1 Nov	All Saints' Day (Munich)
24–26 Dec	Christmas Holiday
31 Dec	New Year's Eve

Hong Kong

1 Jan	New Year's Day
29–31 Jan	Lunar New Year
5 Apr	Ching Ming Festival
14–17 Apr	Easter Holiday
1 May	Labor Day
5 May	Buddha's Birthday
31 May	Tuen Ng Day
1 Jul	SAR Establishment Day
1 Oct	Chinese National Holiday
6 Oct	Mid-Autumn Festival
30 Oct	Chung Yeung Festival
25–26 Dec	Christmas Holiday

India

10 Jan	Bakr-Id (Eid-al-Adha)
26 Jan	Republic Day
31 Jan	Muharram (Islamic New Year)
1 Apr	Half-yearly bank closing
10? Apr	Mahavir Jayanthi
11 Apr	Prophet Muhammad's Birthday
14 Apr	Good Friday
16 Apr	Easter
1 May	Maharashtra Day (Mumbai)
13 May	Buddha Purnima
15 Aug	Independence Day
30 Sep	Half-yearly bank closing
2 Oct	Mahatma Gandhi's Birthday/Dussehra
21 Oct	Diwali (Deepavali)
24 Oct	Ramzan Id (Eid-al-Fitr)
5 Nov	Guru Nanak's Birthday
25 Dec	Christmas
31 Dec	Bakr-Id (Eid-al-Adha)

Additional holidays to be declared

Ireland

1 Jan	New Year's Day
17 Mar	St. Patrick's Day
16–17 Apr	Easter Holiday
1 May	May Day
5 Jun	June Holiday
7 Aug	August Holiday
30 Oct	Halloween
25 Dec	Christmas
26 Dec	St. Stephen's Day

Israel

14 Mar	Purim
13 Apr	First day of Pesach
19 Apr	Last day of Pesach
2 May	Memorial Day
3 May	Independence Day
2 Jun	Shavuot
3 Aug	Fast of Av
23–24 Sep	Rosh Hashanah
2 Oct	Yom Kippur
7 Oct	First day of Sukkot
14–15 Oct	Shemini Atzeret/Simhat Torah

Italy

1 Jan	New Year's Day
6 Jan	Epiphany
16–17 Apr	Easter Holiday
25 Apr	Liberation Day
1 May	Labor Day
2 Jun	Republic Day
29 Jun	Sts. Peter and Paul (Rome)
15 Aug	Assumption Day
1 Nov	All Saints' Day
8 Dec	Immaculate Conception
25 Dec	Christmas
26 Dec	St. Stephen's Day

Japan

1–3 Jan	New Year's Holiday
9 Jan	Coming of Age Day

11 Feb	National Foundation Day
20 Mar	Vernal Equinox Holiday
29 Apr	Greenery Day
3 May	Constitution Day
4 May	National Holiday
5 May	Children's Day
20 Jul	Marine Day
18 Sep	Respect for the Aged Day
23 Sep	Autumnal Equinox Holiday
9 Oct	Health and Sports Day
3 Nov	Culture Day
23 Nov	Labor Thanksgiving Day
23 Dec	Emperor's Birthday
31 Dec	New Year's Eve

Kenya

1 Jan	New Year's Day
14 Apr	Good Friday
16–17 Apr	Easter Holiday
1 May	Labor Day
1 Jun	Madaraka Day
10 Oct	Moi Day
20 Oct	Kenyatta Day
24 Oct	Eid-al-Fitr
12 Dec	Jamhuri Day
25 Dec	Christmas
26 Dec	Boxing Day

Malaysia

1–2 Jan	New Year's Holiday
10 Jan	Hari Raya Haji (Eid-al-Adha)
29–30 Jan	Lunar New Year
31 Jan	Muharram (Islamic New Year)
1 Feb	Federal Territory Day
11 Apr	Prophet Muhammad's Birthday
1 May	Labor Day
13 May	Vesak Day (Buddha's Birthday)
3 Jun	Yang di-Pertuan Agong's Birthday
31 Aug	National Day
21 Oct	Deepavali
24 Oct	Hari Raya Puasa (Eid-al-Fitr)
25 Dec	Christmas
31 Dec	Hari Raya Haji (Eid-al-Adha)

Mexico

1 Jan	New Year's Day
5 Feb	Constitution Day
21 Mar	Benito Juárez' Birthday
13 Apr	Holy Thursday
14 Apr	Good Friday
16 Apr	Easter
1 May	Labor Day
5 May	Battle of Puebla
16 Sep	Independence Day
1 Nov	All Saints' Day
2 Nov	Day of the Dead
20 Nov	Revolution Day
12 Dec	Our Lady of Guadalupe
25 Dec	Christmas

Netherlands

1 Jan	New Year's Day
14 Apr	Good Friday
16–17 Apr	Easter Holiday
30 Apr	Queen's Birthday
5 May	Liberation Day
25 May	Ascension Day
5 Jun	Whitmonday
25–26 Dec	Christmas Holiday

New Zealand

1–3 Jan	New Year's Holiday
23 Jan	Wellington Provincial Anniversary
30 Jan	Auckland Provincial Anniversary
6 Feb	Waitangi Day
14 Apr	Good Friday
16–17 Apr	Easter Holiday
25 Apr	Anzac Day
5 Jun	Queen's Birthday
23 Oct	Labor Day
25 Dec	Christmas
26 Dec	Boxing Day

Puerto Rico

1 Jan	New Year's Day
6 Jan	Three Kings Day (Epiphany)
9 Jan	E. M. de Hostos' Birthday
16 Jan	Martin Luther King Jr. Day
20 Feb	Presidents' Day
22 Mar	Emancipation Day
14 Apr	Good Friday
16 Apr	Easter
17 Apr	José de Diego's Birthday
29 May	Memorial Day
4 Jul	US Independence Day
17 Jul	Luís Muñoz Rivera's Birthday
24 Jul	Constitution Day
27 Jul	José Celso Barbosa's Birthday
4 Sep	Labor Day
12 Oct	Discovery of America
11 Nov	Veterans Day
19 Nov	Discovery of Puerto Rico
23 Nov	Thanksgiving Day
25 Dec	Christmas

Russia

1–3 Jan	New Year's Holiday
7 Jan	Orthodox Christmas
23 Feb	Soldiers' Day
8 Mar	International Women's Day
23 Apr	Orthodox Easter
1–2 May	Labor Day/Spring Holiday
9 May	Victory Day
12 Jun	Independence Day
7 Nov	Day of Accord & Reconciliation
12 Dec	Constitution Day

Saudi Arabia

5–14 Jan	Hajj/Eid-al-Adha
19–28 Oct	Eid-al-Fitr
23 Sep	National Day
26–31 Dec	Hajj/Eid-al-Adha

Business hours reduced during month of Ramadan (Sep–Oct)

Singapore

1–2 Jan	New Year's Holiday
29–31 Jan	Lunar New Year
10 Jan	Hari Raya Haji (Eid-al-Adha)
14 Apr	Good Friday
16 Apr	Easter
1 May	Labor Day
13 May	Vesak Day (Buddha's Birthday)
9 Aug	National Day
21 Oct	Deepavali
24 Oct	Hari Raya Puasa (Eid-al-Fitr)
25 Dec	Christmas
31 Dec	Hari Raya Haji (Eid-al-Adha)

South Africa

1–2 Jan	New Year's Holiday
21 Mar	Human Rights Day
14 Apr	Good Friday
16 Apr	Easter
17 Apr	Family Day
27 Apr	Freedom Day
1 May	Labor Day
16 Jun	Youth Day
9 Aug	National Women's Day
25 Sep	Heritage Day
16 Dec	Day of Reconciliation
25 Dec	Christmas
26 Dec	Day of Goodwill

Spain

1 Jan	New Year's Day
6 Jan	Epiphany
20 Mar	St. Joseph's Day
13 Apr	Holy Thursday
14 Apr	Good Friday
16 Apr	Easter
1 May	Labor Day
15 Aug	Assumption Day
12 Oct	National Holiday
1 Nov	All Saints' Day
6 Dec	Constitution Day
8 Dec	Immaculate Conception
25 Dec	Christmas

Switzerland

1 Jan	New Year's Day
2 Jan	Berchtold's Day
14 Apr	Good Friday
16–17 Apr	Easter Holiday
25 May	Ascension Day
5 Jun	Whitmonday
1 Aug	National Day
25 Dec	Christmas
26 Dec	St. Stephen's Day

2007

JANUARY

s	m	t	w	t	f	s
	1	2	3	4	5	6
7	8	9	10	11	12	13
14	15	16	17	18	19	20
21	22	23	24	25	26	27
28	29	30	31			

FEBRUARY

s	m	t	w	t	f	s
				1	2	3
4	5	6	7	8	9	10
11	12	13	14	15	16	17
18	19	20	21	22	23	24
25	26	27	28			

MARCH

s	m	t	w	t	f	s
				1	2	3
4	5	6	7	8	9	10
11	12	13	14	15	16	17
18	19	20	21	22	23	24
25	26	27	28	29	30	31

APRIL

s	m	t	w	t	f	s
1	2	3	4	5	6	7
8	9	10	11	12	13	14
15	16	17	18	19	20	21
22	23	24	25	26	27	28
29	30					

MAY

s	m	t	w	t	f	s
		1	2	3	4	5
6	7	8	9	10	11	12
13	14	15	16	17	18	19
20	21	22	23	24	25	26
27	28	29	30	31		

JUNE

s	m	t	w	t	f	s
					1	2
3	4	5	6	7	8	9
10	11	12	13	14	15	16
17	18	19	20	21	22	23
24	25	26	27	28	29	30

JULY

s	m	t	w	t	f	s
1	2	3	4	5	6	7
8	9	10	11	12	13	14
15	16	17	18	19	20	21
22	23	24	25	26	27	28
29	30	31				

AUGUST

s	m	t	w	t	f	s
			1	2	3	4
5	6	7	8	9	10	11
12	13	14	15	16	17	18
19	20	21	22	23	24	25
26	27	28	29	30	31	

SEPTEMBER

s	m	t	w	t	f	s
						1
2	3	4	5	6	7	8
9	10	11	12	13	14	15
16	17	18	19	20	21	22
23	24	25	26	27	28	29
30						

OCTOBER

s	m	t	w	t	f	s
	1	2	3	4	5	6
7	8	9	10	11	12	13
14	15	16	17	18	19	20
21	22	23	24	25	26	27
28	29	30	31			

NOVEMBER

s	m	t	w	t	f	s
				1	2	3
4	5	6	7	8	9	10
11	12	13	14	15	16	17
18	19	20	21	22	23	24
25	26	27	28	29	30	

DECEMBER

s	m	t	w	t	f	s
						1
2	3	4	5	6	7	8
9	10	11	12	13	14	15
16	17	18	19	20	21	22
23	24	25	26	27	28	29
30	31					

The CIVIL WAR

Library of Congress

OVER THE COURSE OF four terrible years, the American Civil War took 620,000 lives, devastated large swaths of the South, created streams of refugees, disrupted families and friendships—and redefined the course of the nation. The war decided the two essential questions that sparked it: The United States was, and would ever remain, indivisible. And human slavery could not be countenanced in a country dedicated to the proposition that all men are created equal.

This calendar draws on the unrivaled resources of the Library of Congress to showcase fifty-three Civil War images—contemporary photographs, drawings, and prints; chromolithographs, posters, maps, and documents. Excerpts from letters and diaries offer moving testimony of sacrifice and courage. Concise essays synopsize the war's major figures and its progress on many fronts; wartime events are noted for each day of the year.

Pomegranate

US $14.99 / CANADA $19.99 / UK RRP £10.99 (INC. VAT)

CATALOG NUMBER T223

7 17195 20696 3

ISBN 0-7649-3040-0

51499

9 780764 930409

PRINTED IN KOREA